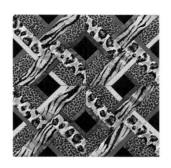

FANCIFUL QUILTS
TO PAPER PIECE

Wendy Vosters

Fanciful Quilts to Paper Piece
© 2005 by Wendy Vosters

That Patchwork Place® is an imprint of Martingale & Company®.

Martingale & Company
20205 144th Avenue NE
Woodinville, WA 98072-8478 USA
www.martingale-pub.com

Credits

President — Nancy J. Martin
CEO — Daniel J. Martin
Publisher — Jane Hamada
Editorial Director — Mary V. Green
Managing Editor — Tina Cook
Technical Editor — Laurie Baker
Copy Editor — Melissa Bryan
Design Director — Stan Green
Illustrator — Laurel Strand
Cover and Text Designer — Shelly Garrison
Studio Photographer — Brent Kane
How-To Photographer — Wendy Vosters

Printed in China
10 09 08 07 06 05   8 7 6 5 4 3 2 1

Library of Congress Cataloging-in-Publication Data

Vosters, Wendy.
    Fanciful Quilts to Paper Piece / Wendy Vosters.
        p. cm.
    ISBN 1-56477-578-X
    1. Patchwork—Patterns. 2. Quilting—Patterns. 3. Netherlands—In art. I. Title.
    TT835.V66 2005
    746.46'041—dc22
                                        2004014849

Acknowledgments

Special thanks to the following people:

My husband, Piet van den Eeden, for his support and for keeping my computer in top condition.

My mother, Topey Vosters, for all her support and for making and testing many of the blocks.

Willy Triviere, Ewing Selcraig, Jessamy Ayad-Thompson, and Luisa Stoop for helping me with my English, and for all of their encouragement.

The Martingale editors for their kind help and guidance. They are a great joy to work with.

Hoffman distributor Ada Honders for writing my foreword and for graciously putting Hoffman fabrics at my disposal.

Colette Keuten for helping me with example photography for Martingale & Company.

Thanks to the following people for all of their support:

My family: Ansje, Willem, Nikki, and Teuntje Vosters.

My friends: Truus Schepers, Else van Veluw, Marina Fluit, Tonnie van Maurik, Margreet Selcraig, Henny van der Haar, Margot Damen, Ankie Koster, Bieke le Clair, Joke Jansen, Bineke van der Haar, Ans van de Boogaard, Mia Stevens, Angela van Nistelrooij, Bep Sanders, and Melanie Schultz.

The members of The Blazing Stars quilt group, De Pientere Pitters quilt group, and all the members of QuiltNed.

Mission Statement
Dedicated to providing quality products and service to inspire creativity.

❀ CONTENTS ❀

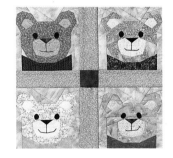

FOREWORD

Wendy Vosters took a beginning quilting class from me in 1995. It soon became obvious that her true strength was not in following someone else's patterns but in designing her own. With her quilting and computer knowledge she has designed many patterns for paper-pieced narrative scenes, each one beautiful and easy to make.

Wendy loves to share her ideas wherever she goes. She is an enthusiastic visitor to the quilting bees, attending every month with her mother. Quilters all over the world are finding out about her ideas and patterns through her Web site, and now even more will be able to enjoy her ideas through this book. In my opinion, this book adds a new dimension to the books already available, but please judge for yourself!

I know Wendy as someone who is always busy with patchwork and quilting. She shares her daily life with her husband, Piet, her mother, and her dogs, and she is always enthusiastic! Patchworkers are social people who enjoy their daily lives. You will find this reflected in these pages. This book shows the stories of everything that happens in day-to-day living, such as dogs and cats lazing around, a wedding ceremony, a piece of Dutch landscape, and a quilt to play on. One thing is certain: this book will spark your enthusiasm and you will spend many happy hours making the quilts in it.

Ada Honders

Quilt Teacher, The Blazing Stars
Organizer of the European Quilt Championships
Distributor of Hoffman Fabrics

❦ INTRODUCTION ❧

Hello, Quilters!

Let me introduce myself . . . Wendy Vosters is my name, and I was born in Holland in 1962.

In 1994 I decided to visit a quilt show, not knowing that it would change my whole life: I was smitten by the patchwork and quilting virus. I especially liked the paper foundation-piecing technique, so it didn't take long before I started drawing my own patterns. Since I am originally a musician, I began by making quilts with designs of musical instruments and symbols. I displayed them on my Web site, and within a year I'd had many Internet visitors from all over the world.

In this book you will find several completed quilts with various themes. But remember that they are just ideas for what you can do with the paper-pieced blocks. Everybody knows that you can make the most beautiful quilts by taking a block from a book, combining it with blocks from other books, finishing it with a block of your own, and ending up with a masterpiece! I urge you all to use the blocks in your own way, make them yours, and be creative. It's much more fun designing something yourself! Of course you can make my examples, but try to give them a personal touch.

Good luck!
Wendy Vosters

The following materials will make it easier for you to complete the projects in this book. Most of them are basic tools and supplies needed for quilting, so if you've done any quilting at all, they are probably already in your sewing room and you can get right to the fun part—sewing!

Fabrics: Use the highest-quality 100%-cotton fabrics that you can afford. Good-quality fabrics are a joy to work with, they don't ravel excessively, and you can get them in many wonderful colors. It is advisable to wash the fabrics before you work with them to find out if you have any colors that may run. In addition, washing the fabrics preshrinks them so the finished quilt will not lose its shape when washed.

Batiks, tone-on-tone prints, and marbled fabrics are most suitable for paper piecing. Avoid large-scale prints with multiple colors so that your quilts do not end up looking too busy.

Threads: Choose good-quality, 100%-cotton sewing thread. A quality thread won't split and you will be able to thread the needle more easily. Cotton thread also won't melt when ironed. Threads are available in a variety of colors, but a neutral color that will blend with all of the fabrics in your project, such as gray, is all you need when paper piecing.

Foundation material: You will need to copy or trace the block patterns onto some sort of foundation material. The foundation is needed so that you have sewing lines to follow and to provide stability while sewing and piecing the blocks together. There are many options that can be used for the foundation, but I prefer either plain copy paper or a lightweight nonfusible interfacing.

Check with your local quilt shop for other options.

Using paper has several advantages. First, you can use a photocopier to transfer the pattern to the paper, which is much easier and quicker than tracing the pattern by hand. Just be aware that distortion can occur, especially around the edges of the copy. Check for any variances by placing the copy on the original pattern and holding them both up to the light. Paper is also easy to remove once the quilt top is complete. The perforations created in the paper each time the needle penetrates the fabric make it easy to tear the paper away at the seam line. Be sure you remove all of the pieces, or when the quilt is washed you may find little balls of paper wandering around inside your quilt.

Lightweight nonfusible interfacing is another foundation option. Unlike paper, the interfacing is not removed; it remains in the quilt, adding a little extra body. The extra layer does make hand quilting more difficult, though, so consider machine quilting if you use interfacing as a foundation.

Sewing machine: Paper piecing requires only a sewing machine that can make a straight stitch. Make sure your sewing machine is in good working order before beginning. Some of the projects call for small pieces to be appliquéd in place; you may do this by machine or by hand, using your favorite method.

Needles: Most quilters prefer to paper piece by machine, but it can be done by hand. If you are machine piecing, start each project with a new needle. If you prefer to piece by hand, work with the sharpest needle you can find so that you can penetrate all of the layers. Appliqué needles are generally sharper than other types of needles.

Rotary-cutting tools: You will need a rotary cutter, mat, and rulers to cut the border pieces and trim the blocks. A long ruler is useful for cutting strips; smaller rulers are available for trimming the block seam allowances.

Pins: Pins are essential for fastening the pieces of fabric temporarily. You will also use them for matching pattern pieces.

Scissors: A pair of sharp, pointed scissors is helpful for trimming threads and cutting small pieces of fabric.

Seam ripper: Even the most experienced paper piecer can make a mistake once in a while.

Iron and ironing surface: Set up an ironing station close to your sewing area because you will need to press each fabric piece in place as it is added to the block. Well-pressed blocks are easier to stitch together and look neater.

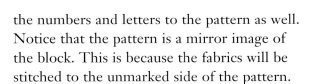

HOW TO PAPER PIECE

The paper-pieced blocks in this book are made up of either a single part (one group of joined segments) or several parts that are sewn together. Each section of the pattern is numbered so that you will know the order in which to add the fabric pieces. For blocks that are made up of multiple parts, each number is preceded by a letter. It doesn't matter in which order you piece these individual parts. For instance, each of the windmills in "Dutch Windmills" on page 12 consists of parts A–E. You can paper piece the segments of part C before you piece part A if you want. What *does* matter is that, once the parts are completed, you sew them together in the order indicated in the instructions.

Follow these steps to piece a single block or to piece each part of a block with multiple parts:

1. Copy or trace the pattern(s) onto the foundation material you have selected. If you are tracing, use a ruler and a pencil so the lines are as straight as possible. Be sure to transfer

the numbers and letters to the pattern as well. Notice that the pattern is a mirror image of the block. This is because the fabrics will be stitched to the unmarked side of the pattern.

2. Make an additional copy of the pattern and cut it apart, following the lines separating each numbered section. Pin each of the numbered sections, number side down, on the right side of the appropriate fabric. Roughly cut around each paper piece, leaving about ½"

of fabric around the pattern. The more excess fabric you have, the easier the paper-piecing process will be.

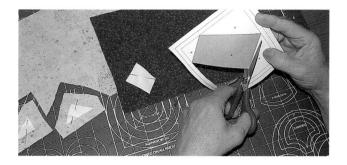

3. If your foundation material is paper or another material that will be removed, set your sewing machine for a short stitch length (approximately 15 to 20 stitches per inch). The smaller the stitch, the easier it is to remove the foundation. If you use a foundation that does not need to be removed, it is also advisable to use a smaller stitch length. When using a smaller stitch, the color of your sewing thread will be invisible; therefore, you can use the same thread for the entire quilt (preferably a neutral color, such as gray).

4. Place the wrong side of the fabric piece that you cut for section 1 on the unmarked side of the whole pattern, making sure the fabric covers section 1 by at least ¼" on all sides. Pin the fabric in place from the marked side. It is easier to position the fabrics if you hold the pattern and the fabric up to a light source.

5. Position the section 2 fabric piece on top of the section 1 fabric piece, right sides together, making sure that one fabric edge extends past the line between sections 1 and 2 by at least ¼". To see if the fabric piece is positioned correctly, pin the fabric in place from the marked side of the pattern directly on the line between sections 1 and 2. Flip the section 2 fabric into place. Section 2 and any adjacent outer edges of the pattern should be completely covered.

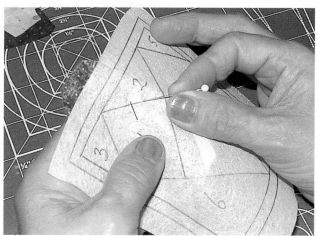

6. Remove the pin from the sewing line and reposition it so that it will not interfere with your stitching. Working from the marked side of the foundation, sew on the line between section 1 and section 2, backstitching at the beginning and end of the line.

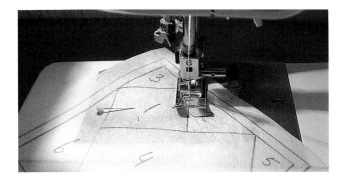

7. Fold the foundation back along the seam line and trim the seam allowance to ¼".

8. From the fabric side, press fabric 2 into place, using either an iron or your fingernail to flatten the seam.

9. Continue adding the remaining fabrics in the same manner, working in numerical order.

10. Trim along the dashed outer edges of the block or part.

REMOVING THE PAPER

Remove the foundation paper after the borders have been stitched to the quilt top. If your quilt top does not have borders, stitch around the outside edges of the quilt top to stabilize the edges, and then remove the paper.

If your block consists of multiple parts:

1. Paper piece each part as described previously.

2. Refer to the project instructions to pin the first two parts together along the seam line. Open up the pieces to be sure they match correctly, and then sew them together using a normal stitch length. If you are in doubt about the accuracy, set your machine for a long stitch length and sew the pieces together temporarily. When you are satisfied, reset your machine for a normal stitch length and sew over the top of the long stitches. It is much easier to rip out long stitches than short ones if the pieces don't match!

3. Press the seams toward the side where fewer fabrics come together, or press them open if there is an excessive amount of bulk.

MIRROR-IMAGE PATTERNS

Throughout the projects I suggest fun ways to use the paper-pieced blocks. Some of these ideas include blocks that are mirror images of blocks used in the featured pattern. To make a mirror-image block, transfer the pattern to the foundation paper as described above, and then turn the paper over and trace the lines. Mark the numbers and, if applicable, the letters for each section along with an *M* to indicate that it is a mirror image.

Finishing a project is one of the best feelings a quilter can have. This section will give you a brief look at the steps involved in completing your quilt so you can share it with others.

ADDING BORDERS

Most of the quilts in this book have easy, straight-cut borders. The lengths to cut the border strips are indicated in the cutting instructions for each project, but these lengths are accurate only if there has been no deviation from the ¼" seam allowance. *Before you cut the strips,* always measure your quilt top and adjust the measurements as needed. Start by measuring through the center of the quilt top from top to bottom; cut two border strips to that length and add them to the sides of the quilt top. Press the seams toward the borders. Measure through the center of the quilt top from side to side, including the borders you just added; cut the border strips to that length and add them to the top and bottom of the quilt top. Press the seams toward the borders.

ASSEMBLING THE LAYERS

After the borders have been added, you are ready to layer the quilt top with backing and batting and baste it all together.

1. Remove any loose threads from the back of your quilt top.

2. Cut your backing fabric approximately 4" larger than the top on all sides. Make sure the grain line of the backing fabric is straight to prevent the quilt from stretching. Lay out the backing, wrong side up, on a large table or on the floor. Smooth out all of the wrinkles, and secure all sides with masking tape.

3. Cut your batting approximately 4" larger than the top on all sides. Place the batting on top of the backing and smooth it out.

4. Center the pieced top, right side up, over the batting and backing and smooth it out. Tape the top in place. It should be taut but not stretched out.

5. Using basting thread and a long needle, baste the layers together, beginning at the center and working toward each corner. Then baste a grid of horizontal and vertical lines 4" to 6" apart. Now you are ready to start quilting!

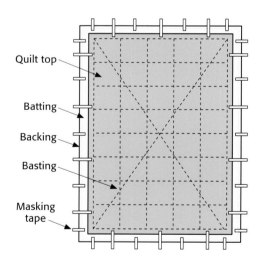

Quilt top

Batting

Backing

Basting

Masking tape

QUILTING

You can quilt by hand or by machine, whichever you prefer and are more comfortable doing. If you have never quilted, there are many good books available for in-depth information on either technique.

If you prefer to machine quilt, just remember to load your bobbin with thread that matches the quilt backing. The creations in this book are mostly pictorial, therefore a mere stitch-in-the-ditch quilting will suffice. Sew right in the seam lines on your quilt top, sewing through all of the layers. Use 100%-cotton or invisible thread for machine quilting. Do not use hand-quilting threads in your machine, as the tiny layer of wax coating makes them unsuitable for sewing machines.

BINDING AND SIGNING

The final step in making your quilt is to bind the raw edges. You're almost done and ready to show off your creation!

1. Trim the backing and batting even with the quilt top.

2. Cut the number of 2¾"-wide strips indicated in the cutting instructions for the project. Cut the strips across the width of the fabric. Stitch the strips together as shown to make one long strip. Press the seams open.

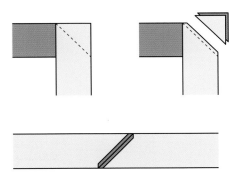

3. Press the strip in half lengthwise, wrong sides together.

4. Press the beginning end of the binding strip up at a 45° angle as shown. Beginning several inches away from a corner of the quilt, pin the doubled binding strip along one edge of the right side of the quilt top, matching raw edges and keeping the beginning fold intact. Stitch the binding to the quilt with a ¼" seam allowance, ending ¼" from the corner. Backstitch and remove the quilt from the machine.

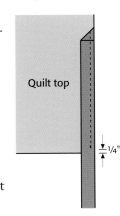

5. Turn the quilt to prepare to sew the next edge. Fold the binding up at a 45° angle as shown. Keeping the angled fold secure, fold the binding back down. This fold should always be parallel with the edge of the quilt top. Beginning at the fold, stitch the binding in place, ending ¼" from the corner. Repeat to sew the remaining corners.

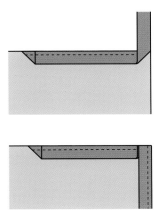

6. When you are within approximately 4" of the starting point, stop stitching. Overlap the end of the binding strip with the beginning of the binding strip about 2". Cut off the excess binding strip and finish stitching the binding to the edge.

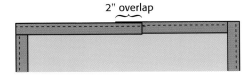

7. Fold the binding over the raw edges of the quilt to the back. Slipstitch the binding in place, mitering the corners.

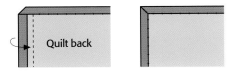

8. Don't forget to sign your quilt!

DUTCH WINDMILLS

A book by a Dutch quilter must include a windmill! In the Netherlands you can still see many of these icons, although not all of them are still in use. The inspiration for this quilt came from an area of the Netherlands called De Zaanse Schans, where many windmills were built next to each other.

Finished quilt size: 27" x 12"

MATERIALS

Yardage is based on 42"-wide fabric.

- 1⅛ yards of black for windmill roof, border, and binding
- ¾ yard of blue for sky
- ¼ yard of green for grass

- ¼ yard of dark brown for windmill upper sections
- ¼ yard of gray or brown for sails
- ⅛ yard of red-and-brown brick print for windmill lower section
- Scrap of light brown for windmill gate
- ⅝ yard of fabric for backing
- 15" x 30" piece of batting

CUTTING

All measurements include ¼"-wide seam allowances.

From the green, cut:

1 strip, 3½" x 4½"

1 strip, 2½" x 5½"

1 strip, 1½" x 6½"

From the black, cut:

4 squares, 3" x 3"

3 strips, 2¾" x 42"

BLOCK ASSEMBLY

1. Copy or trace the foundation patterns from pages 14–18 onto foundation material. Make one copy *each* of parts A–E of all four Windmill block patterns, eight copies of the Top and Bottom Border block pattern, and four copies of the Side Border block pattern.

2. Referring to "How to Paper Piece" on page 7, paper piece parts A–E for the 7", 6", 5", and 4" blocks. Use the illustration and photo below as a guide for fabric placement.

   Assemble the parts of *each* Windmill block as follows:

   Join A to B (AB).

   Join C to D (CD).

   Join AB to CD (ABCD).

   Join ABCD to E.

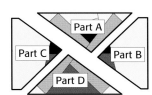

Windmill

3. Paper piece the foundations for the border blocks. Refer to the illustration and photo below for fabric placement to make each combination shown.

| Top Border Block Make 4. | Bottom Border Block Make 4. | Side Border Block Make 3. | Side Border Block Make 1. |

QUILT-TOP ASSEMBLY AND FINISHING

1. Sew the green strips to the bottom of the appropriate blocks; then join the blocks.

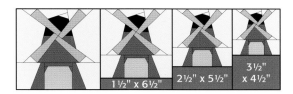

2. Use the border blocks and 3" black squares to assemble the borders as shown.

3. Stitch the side border units and then the top and bottom border units to the quilt top.

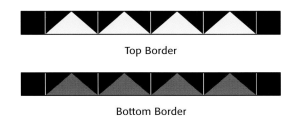

Top Border

Bottom Border

Left Border   Right Border

4. Layer the quilt top with batting and backing; baste. Quilt in the ditch or as desired. Bind the quilt edges with the black strips.

Quilt Assembly Diagram

✢ CREATIVE IDEA ✢

Red-white-and-blue windmills are typical Dutch! The theme is further enhanced with corner blocks that were cut from a fabric featuring Dutch motifs.

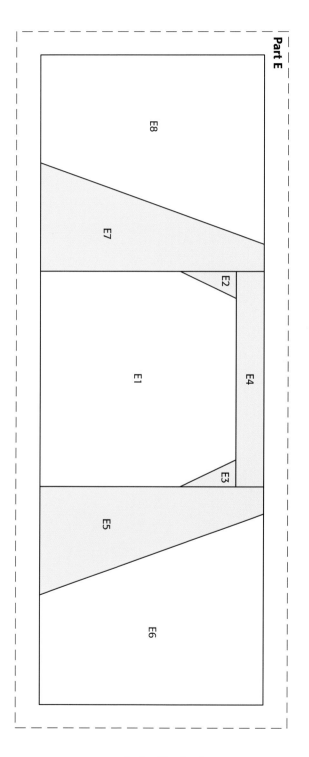

E8

E7

E2

E4

E1

E3

E5

E6

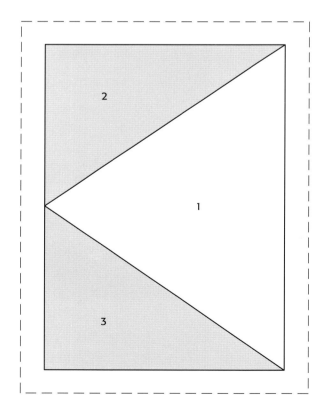

2

1

3

**Side Border Block
Foundation Pattern**

**7" Windmill Block
Foundation Pattern**

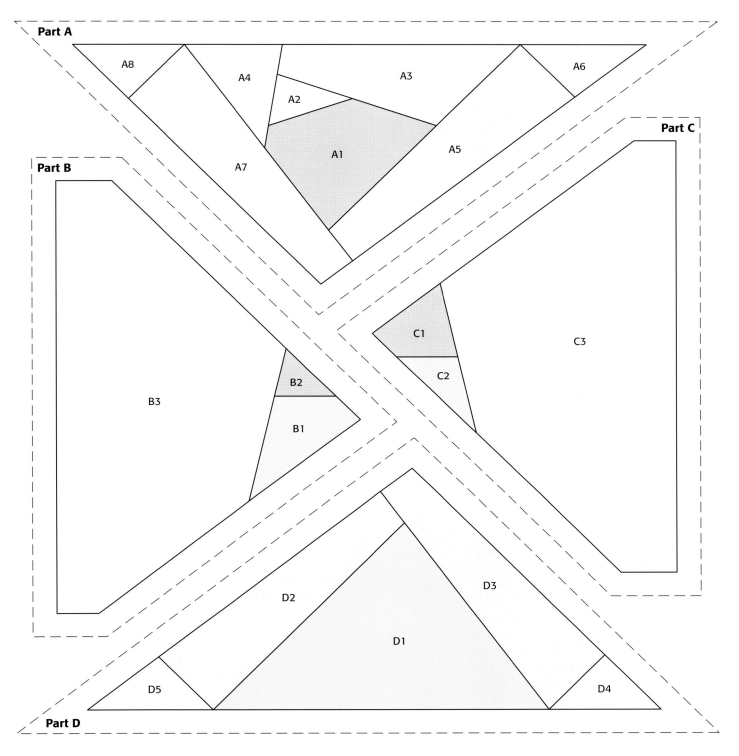

**7" Windmill Block
Foundation Patterns**

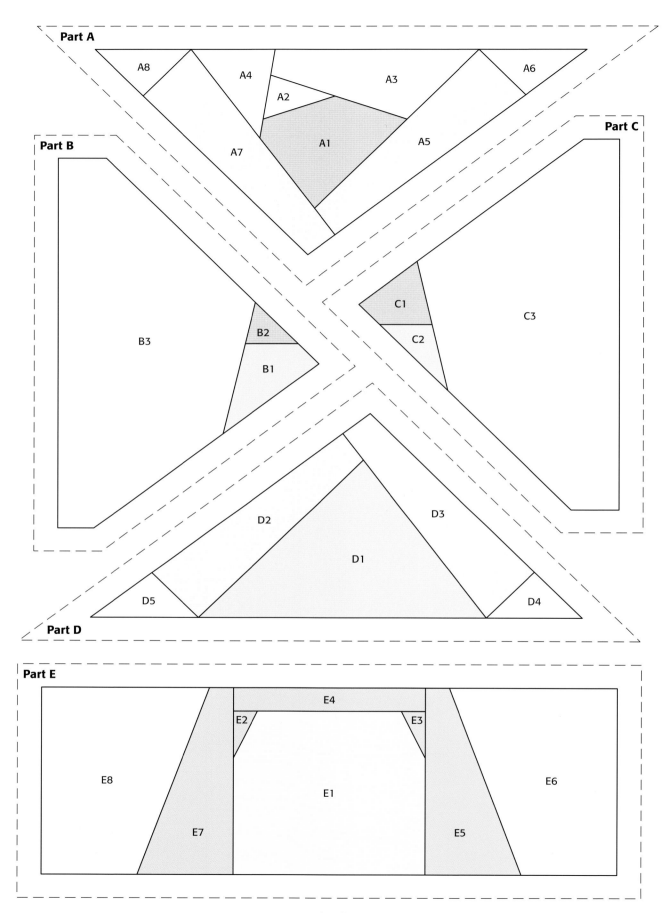

**6" Windmill Block
Foundation Patterns**

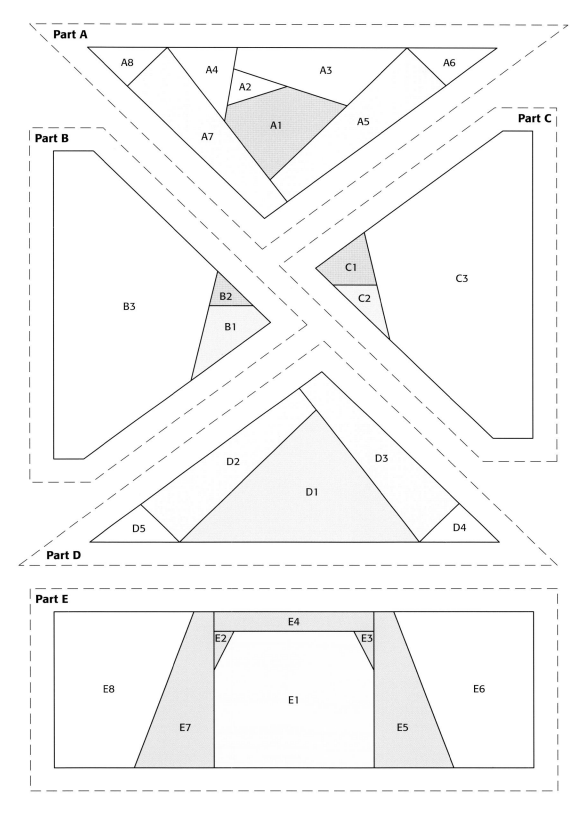

**5" Windmill Block
Foundation Patterns**

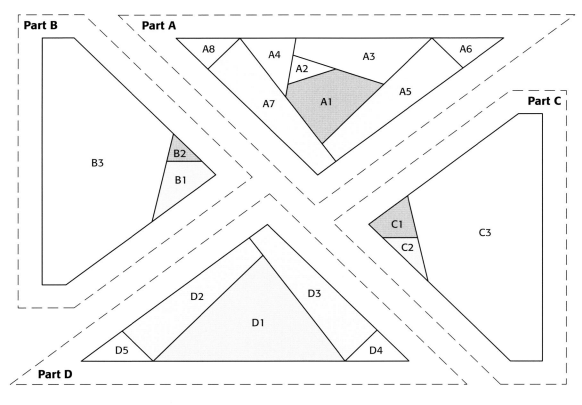

Part B

Part A

A8 · A4 · A2 · A3 · A6 · A7 · A1 · A5

B3 · B2 · B1

Part C

C1 · C2 · C3

D2 · D3 · D1 · D5 · D4

Part D

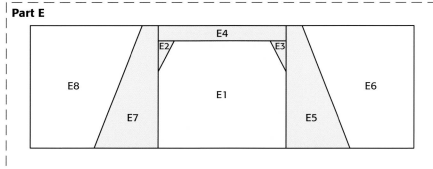

Part E

E4 · E2 · E3 · E8 · E1 · E6 · E7 · E5

**4" Windmill Block
Foundation Patterns**

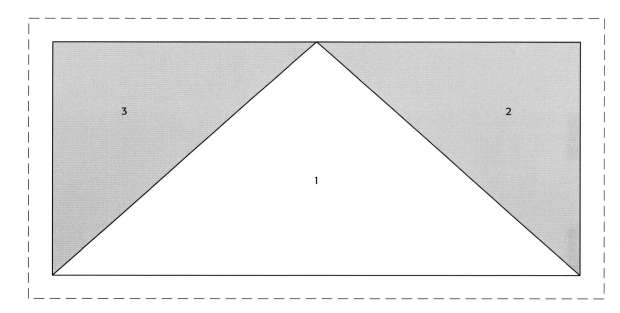

3 · 2 · 1

**Top and Bottom
Border Block
Foundation
Pattern**

I was looking recently for a unique present for my nephew. He loves to play with his toy cars, so I made him this play quilt. It is a kind of street plan of a small village with some houses and a church. He can drive his car around and "visit" places, and then park in the parking lots when he needs a rest. You can also use this quilt as padding for a playpen. When you have finished the quilt, please drive carefully.

Finished quilt size: 42" x 42"
Finished block size: 6" x 6"

MATERIALS

Yardage is based on 42"-wide fabric.

- 3½ yards of green for grass and binding
- 1½ yards of light brown or gray for roads
- Scraps of brown, red, yellow, and blue for houses and church
- 3 yards of fabric for backing
- 46" x 46" piece of batting

CUTTING

All measurements include ¼"-wide seam allowances.

From the green, cut:
5 strips, 2¾" x 42"

BLOCK ASSEMBLY

1. Copy or trace the foundation patterns from pages 22–30 onto foundation material. Make the following number of each pattern:

House 1	10
House 2	3 *each* of parts A–C
Church	1 *each* of parts A and B
Road 1	12
Road 2	4
Road 3	7 *each* of parts A and B
Road 4	5
Road 5	5
Parking Lot	2

2. Referring to "How to Paper Piece" on page 7, paper piece the foundations for each House 1 block; each Road 1, 2, 4, and 5 block; and each Parking Lot block. Use the illustrations as a guide for fabric placement.

3. Paper piece the foundations for parts A–C of each House 2 block, referring to the illustration for fabric placement. Join the parts as follows:

Join B to C (BC).

Join BC to A.

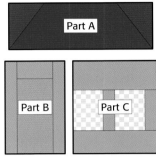

House 2

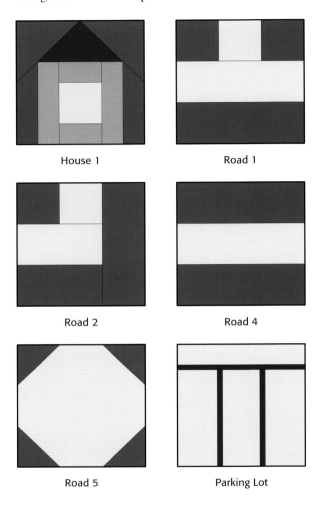

House 1

Road 1

Road 2

Road 4

Road 5

Parking Lot

4. Paper piece the foundations for parts A and B of the Church block, referring to the illustration for fabric placement. Join part A to part B as shown.

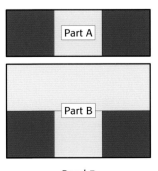

Church

5. Paper piece the foundations for parts A and B of each Road 3 block, referring to the illustration for fabric placement. Join part A to part B as shown.

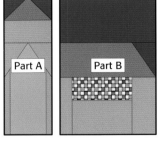

Road 3

Just look at all the designs you can create with the House and Road block patterns from this quilt.

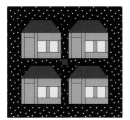

House 2 Blocks

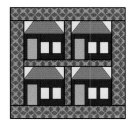

House 2 Blocks

Road 1 Blocks

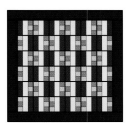

Road 1 Blocks

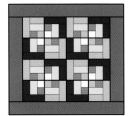

Road 2 Blocks

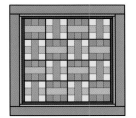

Road 3 Blocks

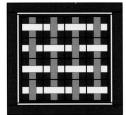

Road 3 Blocks

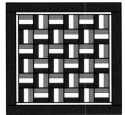

Road 4 Blocks

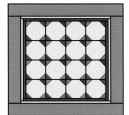

Road 5 Blocks

QUILT-TOP ASSEMBLY AND FINISHING

1. Arrange the blocks into seven horizontal rows as shown. Stitch the blocks in each row together, and then stitch the rows together.

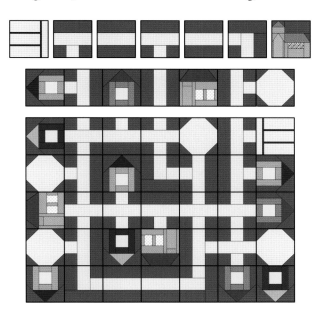

2. Layer the quilt top with batting and backing; baste. Quilt in the ditch or as desired. Bind the quilt edges with the green strips.

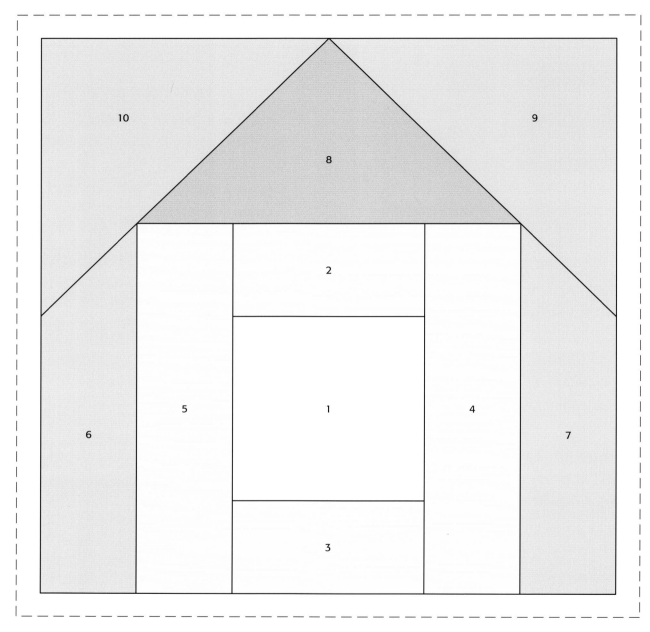

House 1 Block
Foundation Pattern

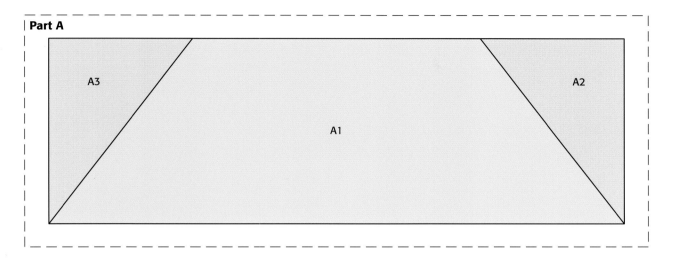

Part A

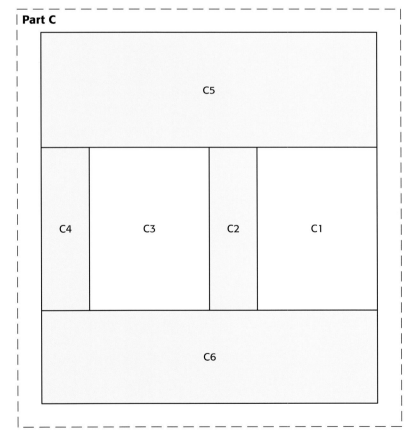

Part C

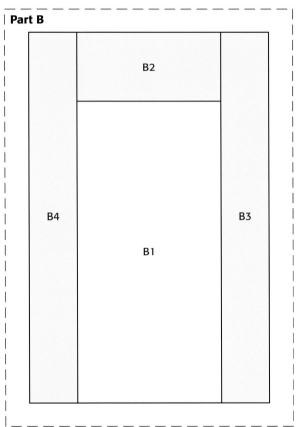

Part B

**House 2 Block
Foundation Patterns**

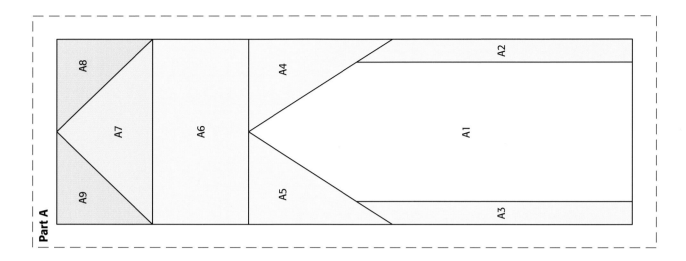

Part A

A8
A7
A9
A6
A4
A5
A2
A1
A3

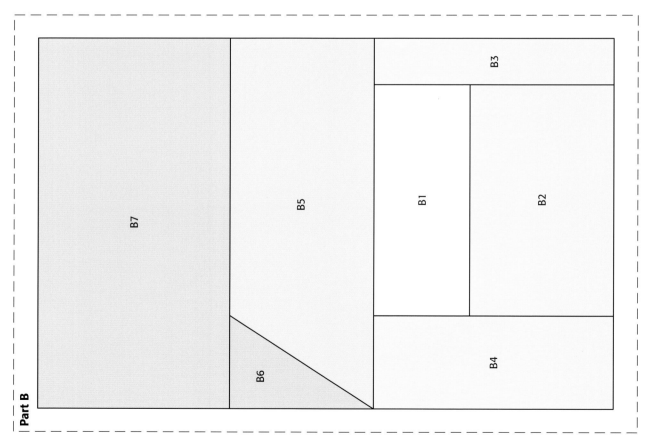

Part B

B7
B5
B6
B1
B2
B3
B4

**Church Block
Foundation Patterns**

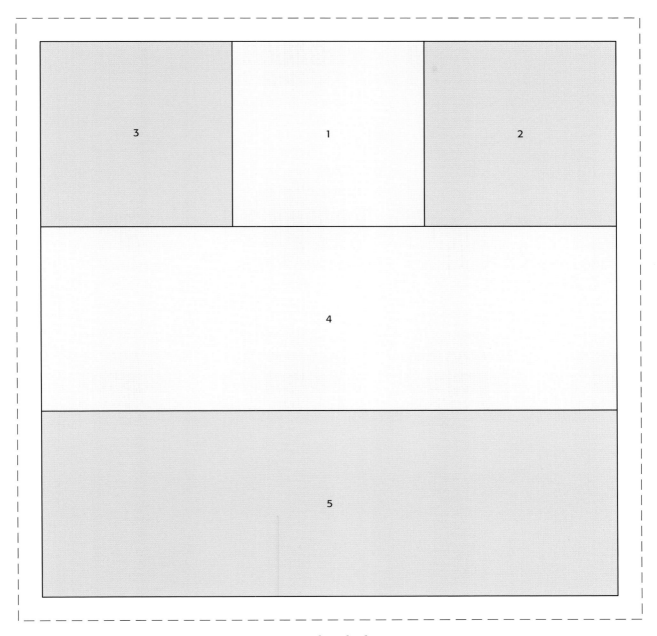

Road 1 Block
Foundation Pattern

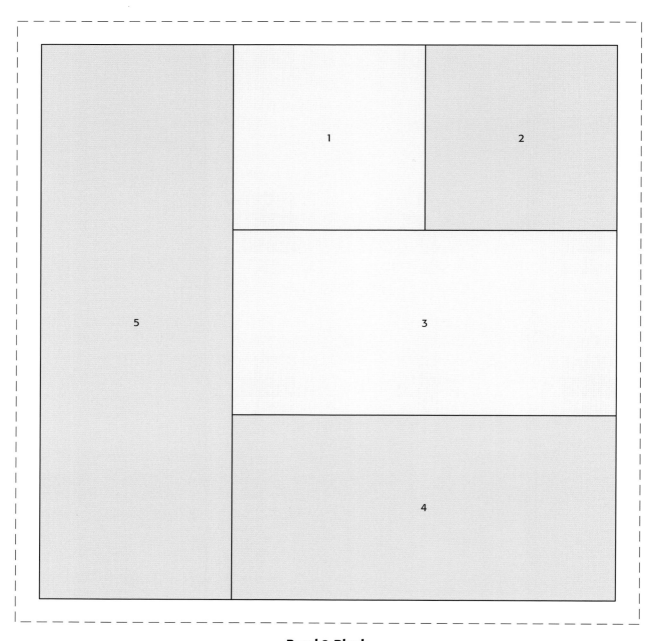

Road 2 Block
Foundation Pattern

Part A

A3	A1	A2

Part B

B4		
B3	B1	B2

**Road 3 Block
Foundation Patterns**

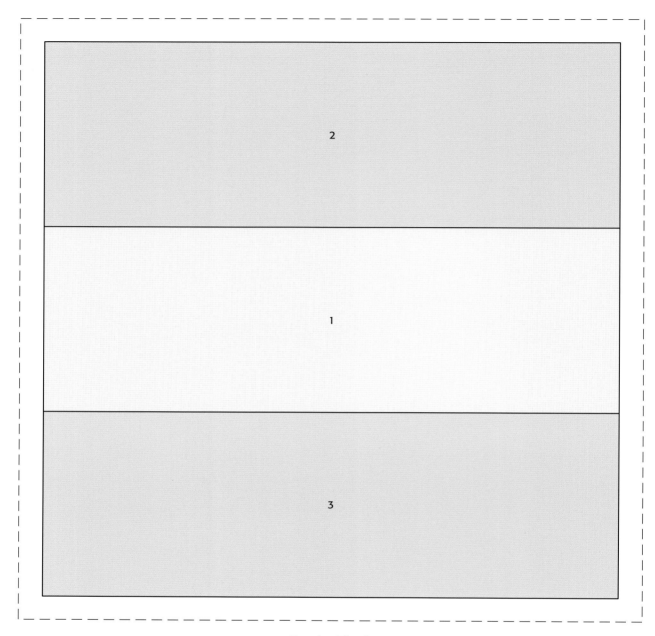

Road 4 Block
Foundation Pattern

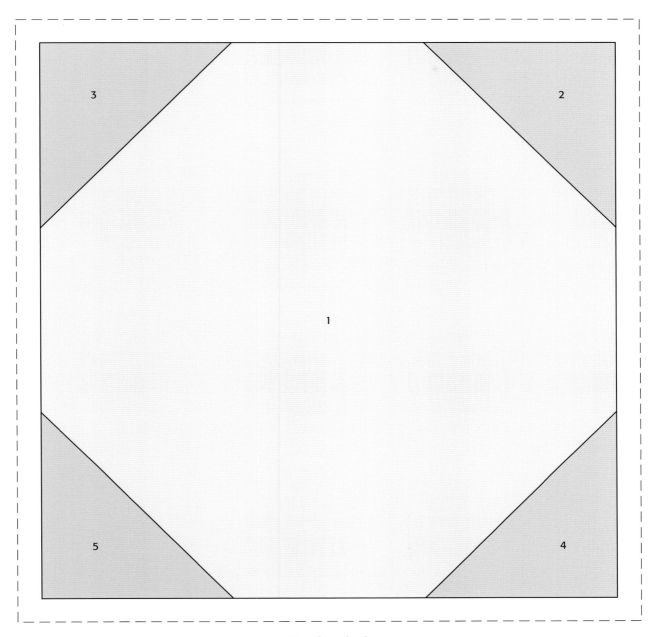

**Road 5 Block
Foundation Pattern**

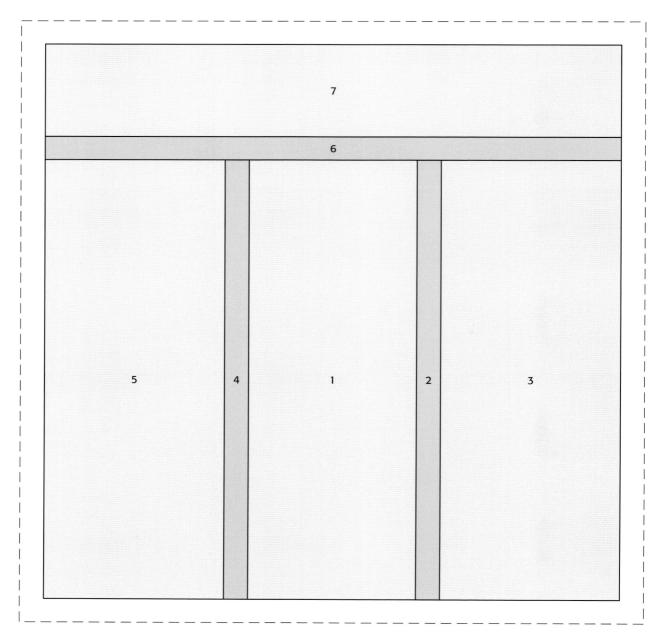

Parking Lot Block
Foundation Pattern

Finished quilt size: 23" x 28"
Finished Bride-and-Groom block size:
  9" x 14"
Finished Champagne Flutes block size:
  4" x 6"
Finished Bouquet block size: 6" x 6"
Finished Cake block size: 4" x 8"
Finished Bells block size: 9" x 4"
Finished Large Heart block size: 2" x 2"
Finished Small Heart block size: 1" x 1"

MATERIALS

Yardage is based on 42"-wide fabric.

- 1¾ yards of cream for background
- ⅞ yard of dark print for border and binding
- ¼ yard of white satin for dress
- ¼ yard of white cotton for veil, champagne flutes, and cake
- ¼ yard of black for coat, hat, and bell clappers
- ¼ yard of red for hearts
- ⅛ yard of gray for bells, bouquet handle, and cake towers
- ⅛ yard of floral print for bouquet
- Scraps of two different dark grays for coat sleeve and trousers
- Scraps of two different flesh tones for groom's skin and bride's skin
- Scraps of light and dark pink for cake
- Scraps of two different yellows for bell and bouquet ribbons
- Scrap of gold for champagne
- Scrap of green for bouquet
- 1 yard of fabric for backing
- 27" x 32" piece of batting

Every quilter will make a quilt as a gift at least once, usually for a special occasion such as a wedding. I designed this quilt when a member of my family was getting married and I couldn't find any wedding-related paper-piecing patterns. For the dress in the quilt, I even used scraps that were left over from the making of my own wedding dress! You can also make this quilt for a twenty-fifth or fiftieth wedding anniversary. Just add the couple's initials or embroider the date on the quilt, and success is ensured!

CUTTING

All measurements include ¼"-wide seam allowances.

From the cream, cut:

2 squares, 2½" x 2½"

From the dark print, cut:

2 strips, 4½" x 20½"

2 strips, 4½" x 23½"

3 strips, 2¾" x 42"

BLOCK ASSEMBLY

1. Copy or trace the foundation patterns from pages 35–43 onto foundation material. Make one copy *each* of parts A–K of the Bride-and-Groom block, parts A–F of the Champagne Flutes block, parts A–D of the Bouquet block, parts A–F of the Cake block, and parts A–I of the Bells block. Make nine copies of the Large Heart block and two copies of the Small Heart block.

2. Referring to "How to Paper Piece" on page 7, paper piece the foundations for parts A–D and F–K of the Bride-and-Groom block. Use the illustration as a guide for fabric placement. Part E is not foundation pieced; lay the foundation for part E on the wrong side of the appropriate fabric and cut out the triangle on the outer dashed lines. Discard the foundation. Join the parts as follows:

   Join B to C (BC).

   Join BC to D (BCD).

   Join F to G (FG).

   Join H to I (HI).

   Join FG to HI (FGHI).

   Join BCD to FGHI (BCDFGHI).

   Join BCDFGHI to E (BCDEFGHI).

   Join A to BCDEFGHI (ABCDEFGHI).

   Join J to K (JK).

   Join ABCDEFGHI to JK.

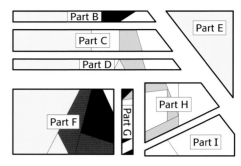
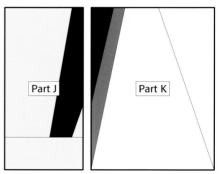
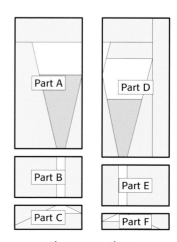

Bride and Groom

3. Paper piece the foundations for parts A–F of the Champagne Flutes block, referring to the illustration for fabric placement. Join the parts as follows:

   Join A to B (AB).

   Join AB to C (ABC).

   Join D to E (DE).

   Join DE to F (DEF).

   Join ABC to DEF.

Champagne Flutes

- I used the top part of the happy couple for a little ring pillow. Attach a ribbon to the left and right sides to tie the rings in place. The dress fabric was left over from the making of my own wedding gown. The veil has two layers: first a layer of quilting fabric and then a piece of leftover material from my wedding veil, which I sewed on at the same time as the quilting fabric. This will make a lovely memento of the beginning of any couple's marriage!

- Enlarge the Champagne Flutes block patterns 200% to create a celebratory small quilt for anniversaries, birthdays, and, of course, the new year.

4. Paper piece the foundations for parts A–D of the Bouquet block, referring to the illustration for fabric placement. Join the parts as follows:

   Join A to B (AB).

   Join AB to C (ABC).

   Join ABC to D.

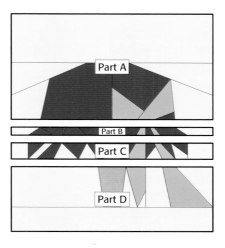

5. Paper piece the foundations for parts A–F of the Cake block, referring to the illustration for fabric placement. Join the parts as follows:

   Join A to B (AB).

   Join AB to C (ABC).

   Join ABC to D (ABCD).

   Join ABCD to E (ABCDE).

   Join ABCDE to F.

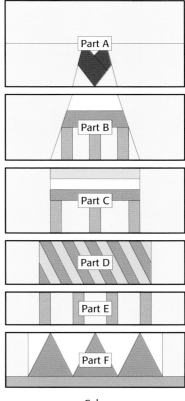

Cake

6. Paper piece the foundations for parts A–I of the Bells block, referring to the illustration for fabric placement. Join the parts as follows:

Join A to B (AB).

Join C to D (CD).

Join AB to CD (ABCD).

Join E to F (EF).

Join EF to G (EFG).

Join H to I (HI).

Join EFG to HI (EFGHI).

Join ABCD to EFGHI.

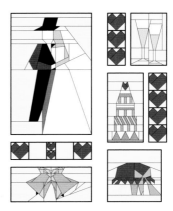

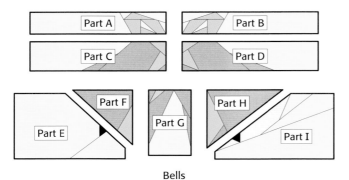

Bells

7. Paper piece the foundations for the nine large hearts and the two small hearts, referring to the illustration for fabric placement.

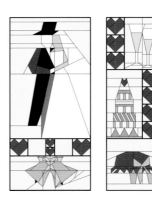

Heart

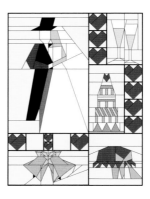

QUILT-TOP ASSEMBLY AND FINISHING

1. Arrange the foundation-pieced blocks and the cream 2½" squares into units as shown at right. Stitch the units with heart blocks together. Stitch the units in each vertical half together as shown, and then stitch the halves together.

2. If desired, embroider or appliqué the initials of the bride and groom on the two cream 2½" squares, using your favorite method.

3. Referring to "Adding Borders" on page 10 and the quilt assembly diagram, sew the dark print 4½" x 20½" strips to the sides of the

quilt top, and then sew the dark print 4½" x 23½" strips to the top and bottom of the quilt top.

Quilt Assembly Diagram

4. Layer the quilt top with batting and backing; baste. Quilt in the ditch or as desired. Bind the quilt edges with the dark print 2¾"-wide strips.

❋ CREATIVE IDEA ❋

Toss the Bouquet block together with several Large Heart blocks for an affectionate reminder to your family that Valentine's Day is drawing near. Enlarge each of the block patterns 200%.

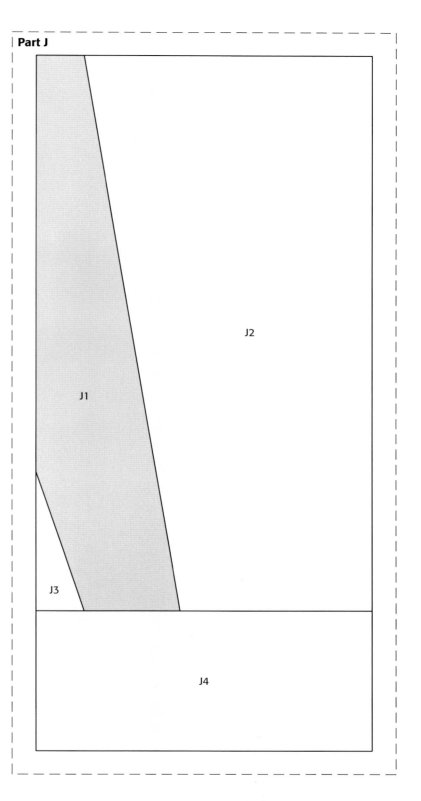

Bride and Groom Block
Foundation Pattern

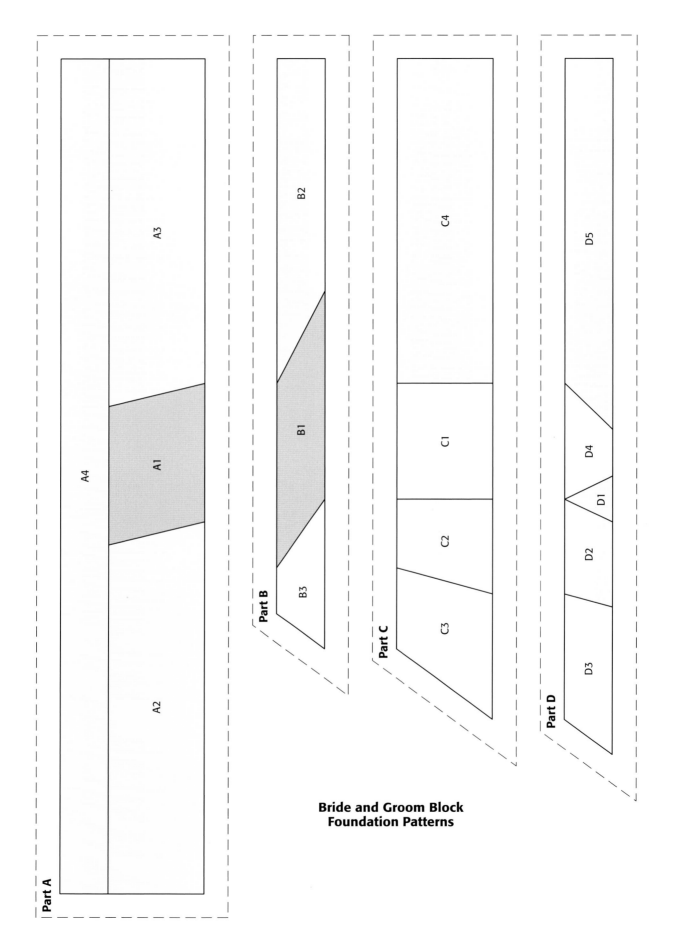

**Bride and Groom Block
Foundation Patterns**

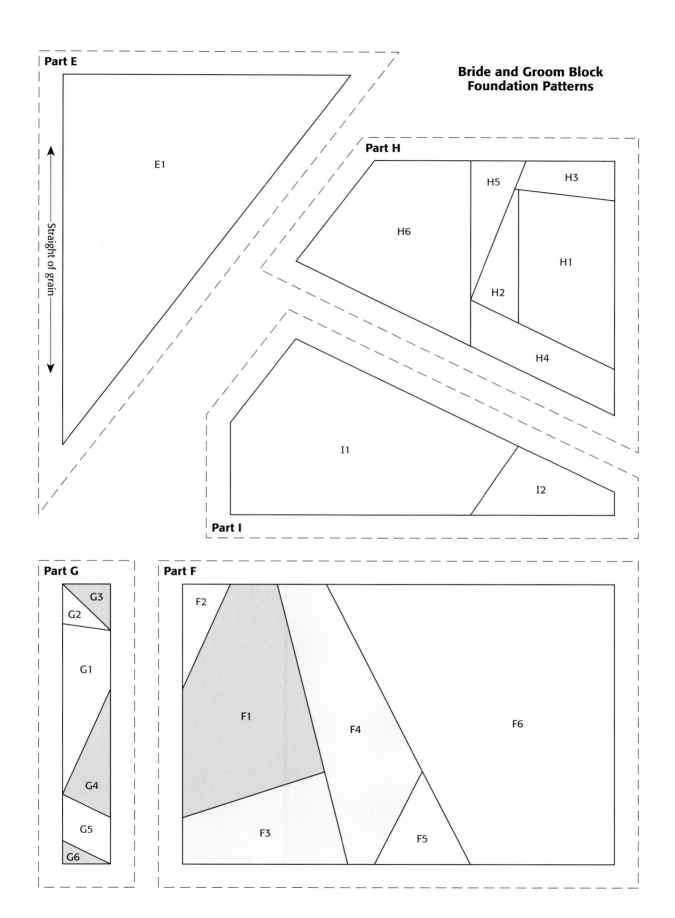

Part E

Straight of grain

E1

**Bride and Groom Block
Foundation Patterns**

Part H

H5   H3

H6   H1

H2

H4

Part I

I1

I2

Part G

G3
G2
G1
G4
G5
G6

Part F

F2

F1   F4   F6

F3   F5

Part K

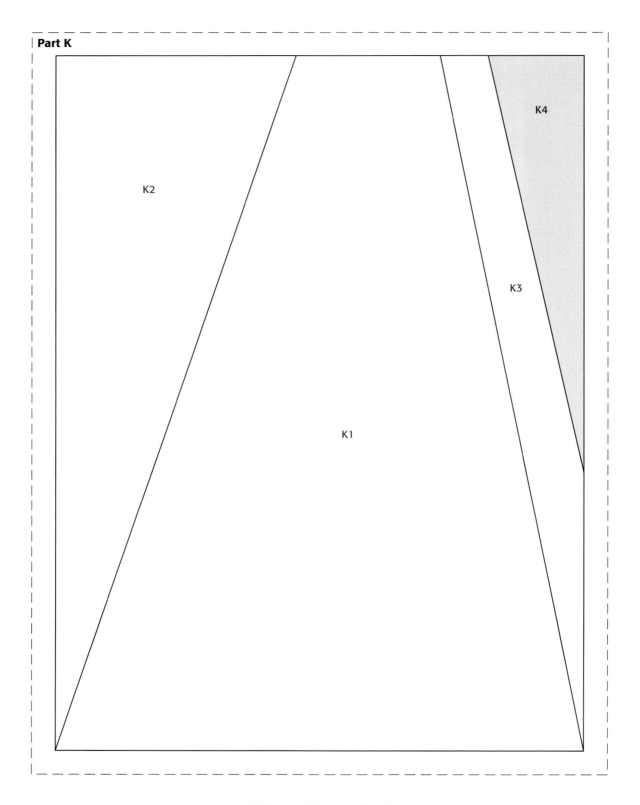

**Bride and Groom Block
Foundation Pattern**

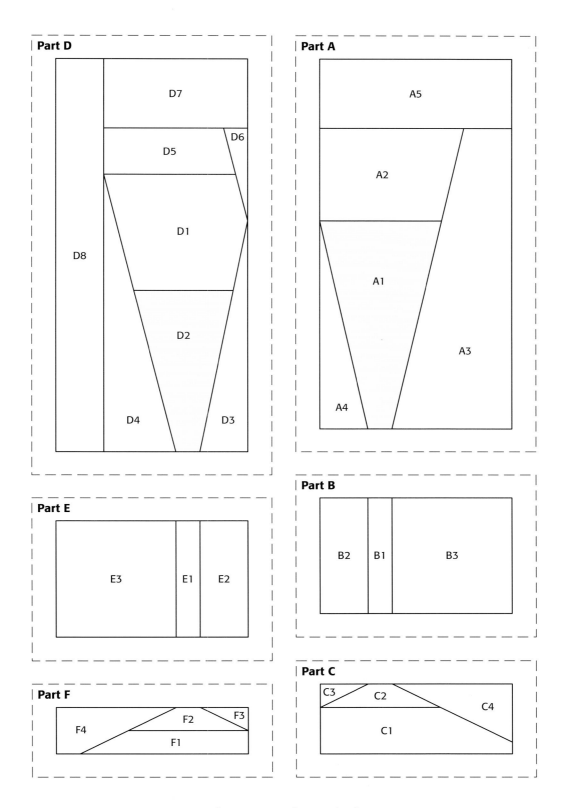

**Champagne Flutes Block
Foundation Patterns**

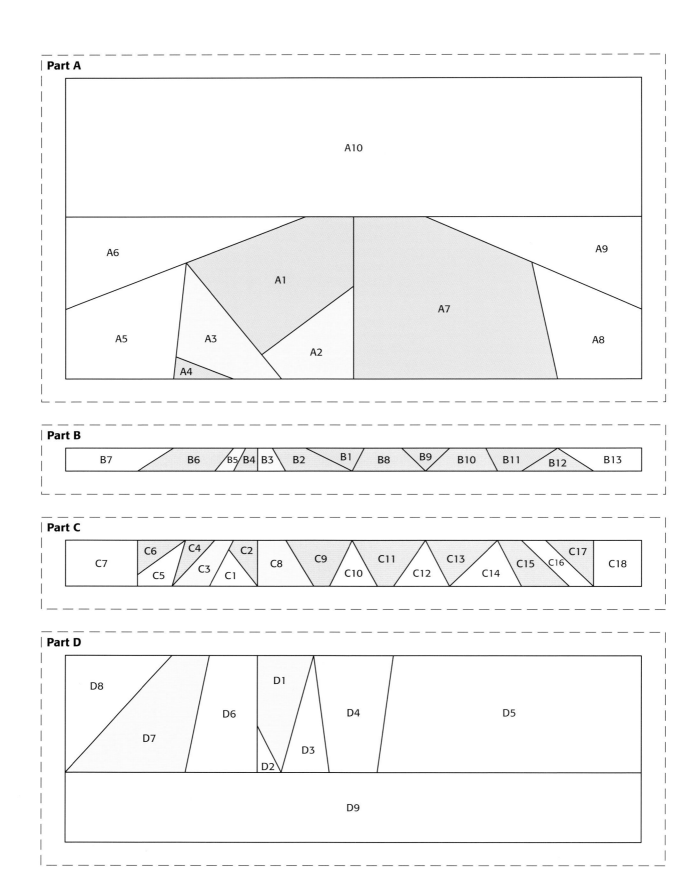

**Bouquet Block
Foundation Patterns**

Cake Block
Foundation Patterns

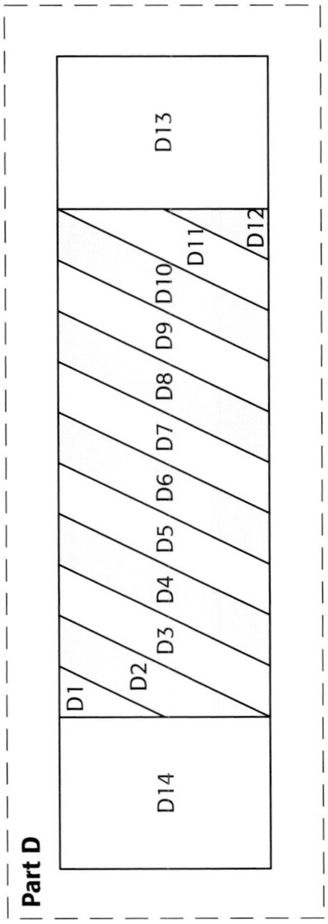

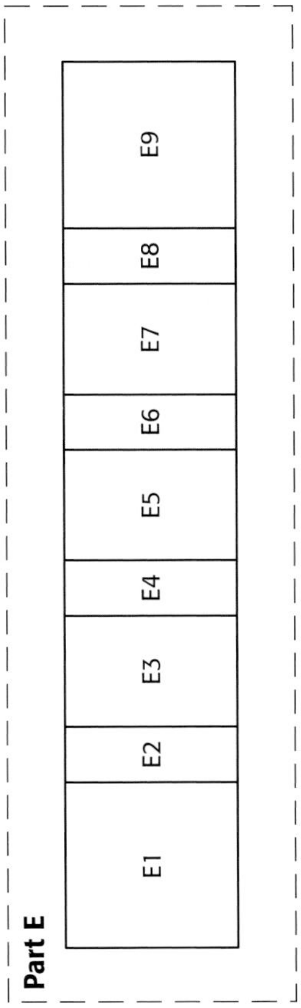

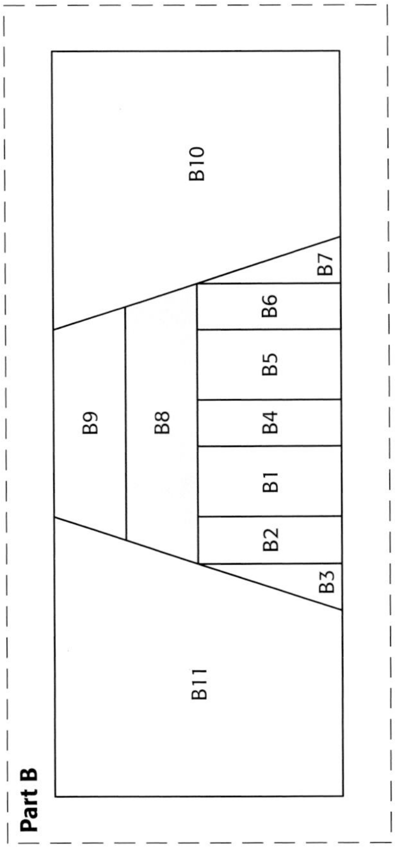

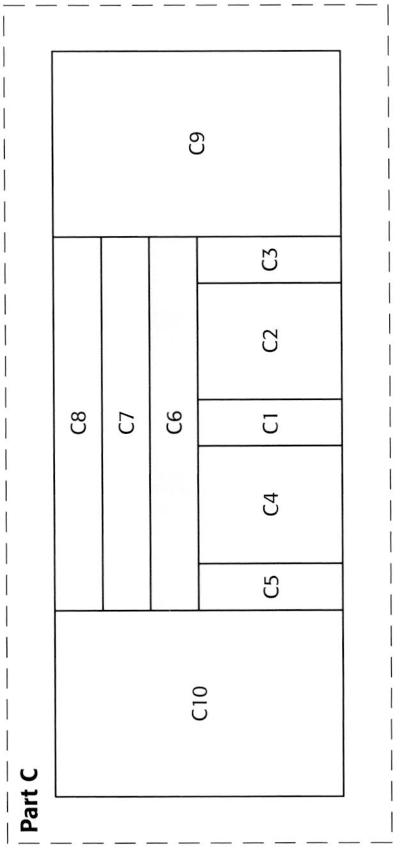

Part A

A8

A7

A2 A3
A1
A4
A5

A6

Part B

B10

B9

B8

B6
B5
B4 B7
B1
B2
B3

B11

Part C

C9

C8
C7
C6

C3
C2
C1
C4
C5

C10

Part D

D13

D1
D2
D3 D4 D5 D6 D7 D8 D9 D10
D11
D12

D14

Part E

E9
E8
E7
E6
E5
E4
E3
E2
E1

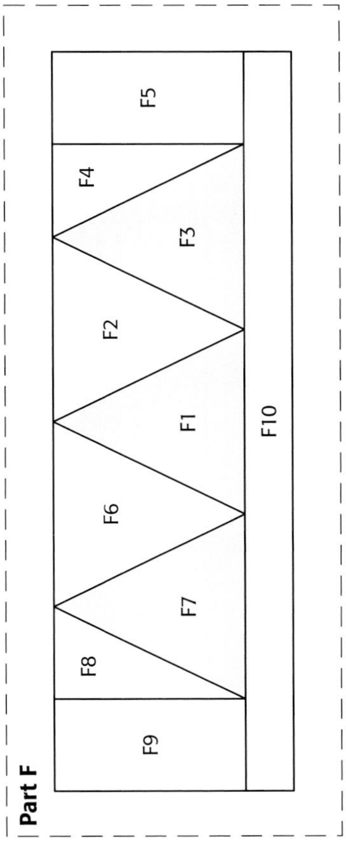

Part F

F5
F4
F3
F2
F1
F6
F7
F8
F9
F10

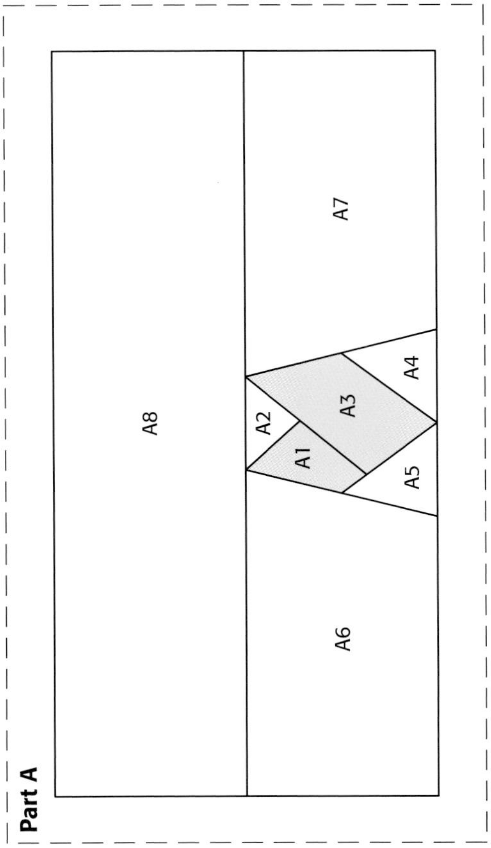

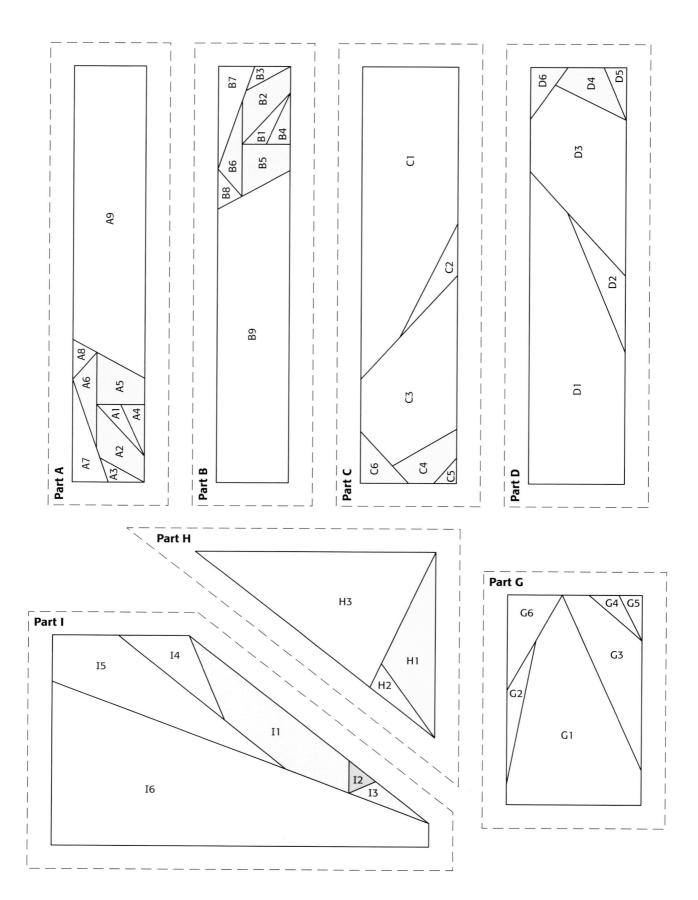

**Bells Block
Foundation Patterns**

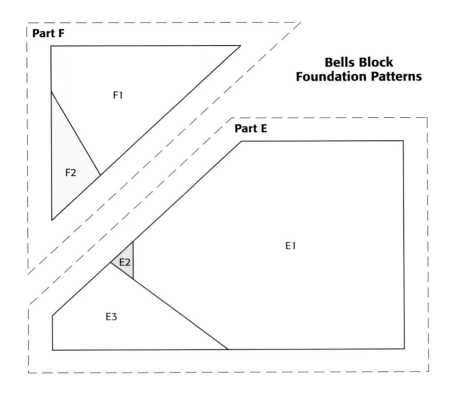

Part F

F1

F2

**Bells Block
Foundation Patterns**

Part E

E1

E2

E3

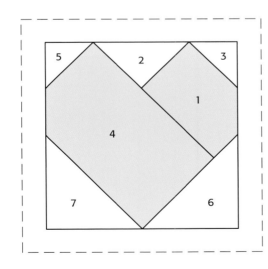

5   2   3

1

4

7   6

**Large Heart Block
Foundation Pattern**

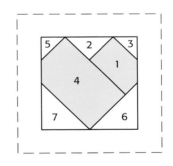

5   2   3

1

4

7   6

**Small Heart Block
Foundation Pattern**

This rose quilt is one of my favorites! The beautiful reds on the cream background just emanate warmth, and there are so many different ways you can arrange several of these blocks together.

Finished quilt size: 22" x 22"
Finished block size: 7" x 7"

MATERIALS

Yardage is based on 42"-wide fabric.

- 1⅛ yards of cream for background
- ¾ yard of rose print for border and binding
- ¼ yard of green for leaves and stems
- Scraps of assorted light, medium, and dark reds for roses
- ⅞ yard of fabric for backing
- 26" x 26" piece of batting

CUTTING

All measurements include ¼"-wide seam allowances.

From the rose print, cut:
2 strips, 4½" x 14½"
2 strips, 4½" x 22½"
3 strips, 2¾" x 42"

BLOCK ASSEMBLY

1. Copy or trace the foundation patterns from pages 47 and 48 onto foundation material twice each.

2. Referring to "How to Paper Piece" on page 7, paper piece the foundations for the two Rose blocks. Use the illustration as a guide for fabric placement. To

create a more lifelike rose, select the light, medium, and dark reds randomly when piecing each flower.

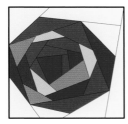
Rose

3. Paper piece the foundations for parts A and B of the two Stem blocks, referring to the illustration for fabric placement. Join each part A to a part B as shown.

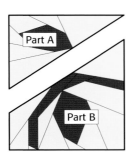
Stem

QUILT-TOP ASSEMBLY AND FINISHING

1. Arrange the blocks into two horizontal rows as shown. Stitch the blocks in each row together, and then stitch the rows together.

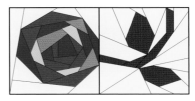

2. Referring to "Adding Borders" on page 10 and the quilt assembly diagram, sew the rose print 4½" x 14½" strips to the sides of the quilt top, and then sew the rose print 4½" x 22½" strips to the top and bottom of the quilt top.

Quilt Assembly Diagram

3. Layer the quilt top with batting and backing; baste. Quilt in the ditch or as desired. Bind the quilt edges with the rose print 2¾"-wide strips.

- Paper piece eight Rose and eight Stem blocks and your rose garden will be in full bloom all year long.

- Make a mirror-image pattern of the Rose and Stem block foundations. Here are some ideas for combining the two images.

Pin your birthday cards to this rose-topped holder.

A table runner in country colors would be nice!

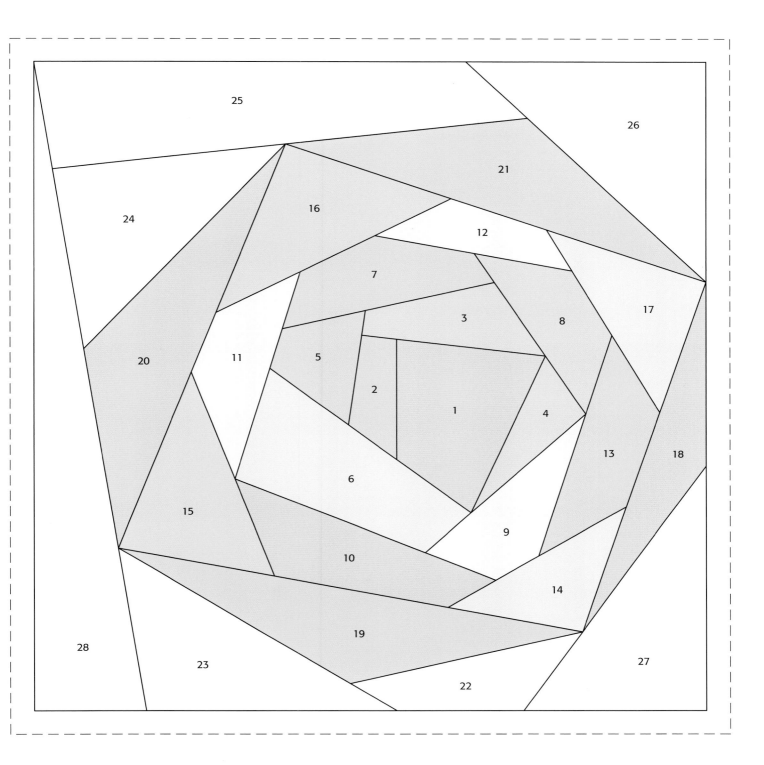

**Rose Block
Foundation Pattern**

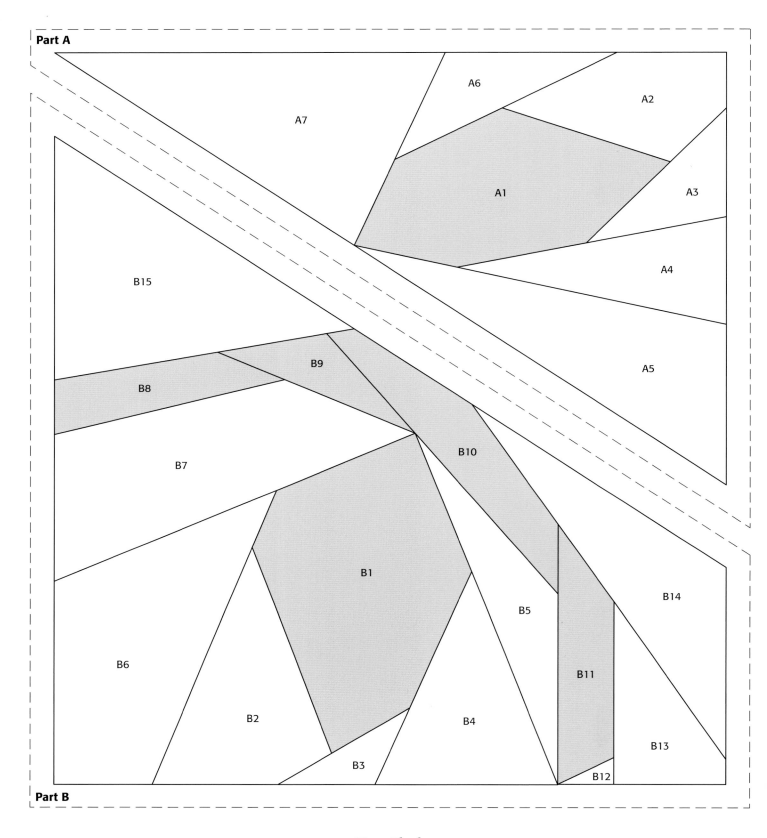

Part A

A6

A2

A7

A1

A3

A4

A5

B15

B9

B8

B7

B10

B1

B5

B14

B6

B11

B2

B4

B3

B12

B13

Part B

**Stem Block
Foundation Patterns**

Wild animal prints . . . I just love them! As long as I can remember, I've wanted to make a quilt with animal-print fabrics. It had to be something simple that would show off the print itself. Finally, I came up with this quilt. It has only one pattern, but you use four foundations to make each block. Be very careful to follow the fabric placement so that the vividly colored diamonds will appear.

Finished quilt size: 30" x 30"
Finished block size: 6" x 6"

MATERIALS

Yardage is based on 42"-wide fabric.

- 2 yards of black for blocks, inner and outer borders, and binding
- ¾ yard of bright red for blocks and middle border
- ½ yard of light animal print for blocks
- ½ yard of medium-dark animal print for blocks
- ½ yard of white-and-gray animal print for blocks
- ¼ yard of bright yellow for blocks
- ¼ yard of bright green for blocks
- ¼ yard of bright blue for blocks
- 1 yard of fabric for backing
- 34" x 34" piece of batting

CUTTING

All measurements include ¼"-wide seam allowances.

From the black, cut:
2 strips, 1" x 18½"
2 strips, 1" x 19½"
2 strips, 5½" x 20½"
2 strips, 5½" x 30½"
4 strips, 2¾" x 42"

From the red, cut:
2 strips, 1" x 19½"
2 strips, 1" x 20½"

BLOCK ASSEMBLY

1. Copy or trace the foundation pattern from page 51 onto foundation material 36 times.

2. Referring to "How to Paper Piece" on page 7, paper piece the foundations. Use the illustrations as a guide for fabric placement. Make the number shown for each fabric combination.

Make 5.   Make 5.

Make 5.   Make 5.

Make 4.   Make 4.

Make 4.   Make 4.

3. Arrange the triangles as shown to make the two different blocks. For each block, stitch two adjacent triangles together and then join the two pairs of triangles. Make the number of blocks shown for each combination.

Make 5.   Make 4.

QUILT-TOP ASSEMBLY AND FINISHING

1. Arrange the blocks into three horizontal rows as shown, rotating the blocks as needed to achieve the pattern. Stitch the blocks in each row together, and then stitch the rows together.

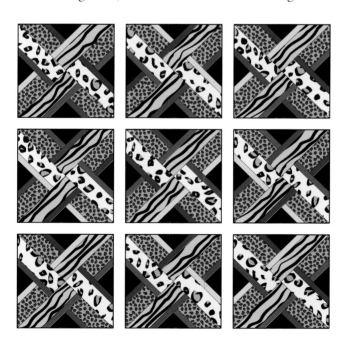

2. Referring to "Adding Borders" on page 10 and the quilt assembly diagram, stitch the borders to the quilt top. For the inner border, sew the black 1" x 18½" strips to the sides of the quilt top, and then sew the black 1" x 19½" strips to the top and bottom of the quilt top. For the middle border, sew the red 1" x 19½" strips to the sides of the quilt top, and then sew the red 1" x 20½" strips to the top and bottom of the quilt top. For the outer border, sew the black 5½" x 20½" strips to the sides of the quilt top, and then sew the black 5½" x 30½" strips to the top and bottom of the quilt top.

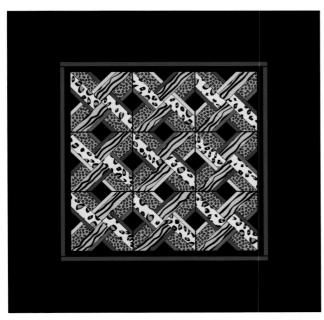

Quilt Assembly Diagram

3. Layer the quilt top with batting and backing; baste. Quilt in the ditch or as desired. Bind the quilt edges with the black 2¾"-wide strips.

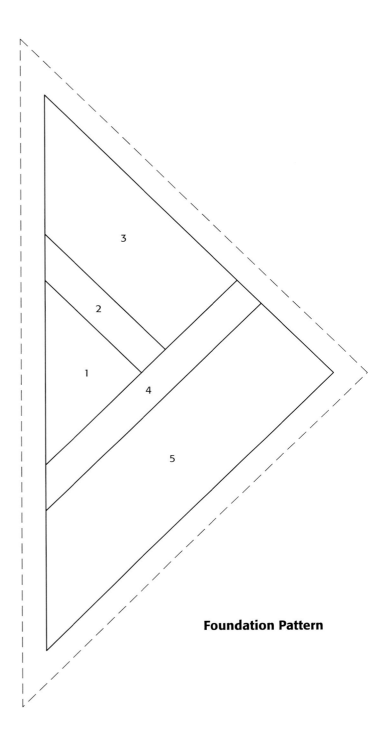

Foundation Pattern

Finished quilt size: 26½" x 30½"
Finished Dog 1 block size: 6" x 8"
Finished Food Bowl block size: 6" x 4"
Finished Dog 2 block size: 6" x 6"
Finished No! block size: 6" x 2"
Finished Dog 3 block size: 10" x 6"
Finished Dog 4 block size: 8" x 8"
Finished Paw block size: 2" x 8"
Finished Dog 5 block size: 10" x 6"
Finished Dog Bone block size: 5" x 5"

MATERIALS

Yardage is based on 42"-wide fabric.

- 1¼ yards of black for blocks, inner border, outer-border corner squares, and binding
- 1 yard of blue for sky
- ¾ yard of green for grass
- ⅝ yard of brown for outer border
- ⅜ yard of red-brown for dogs
- ¼ yard of cream for bones
- ¼ yard of gray-brown for dogs
- ¼ yard of dark brown for dogs
- ¼ yard of light brown for dogs
- ¼ yard of yellow for sun and letters
- ⅛ yard of brown woven print for dog bed
- Scraps of light gray and dark gray for garbage can
- Scraps of beige for ears and bowl
- Scraps of brown and yellow for bowl
- 1 yard of fabric for backing
- 31" x 35" piece of batting

I have four dogs at home, so with that much inspiration running around, how could I not make a dog quilt? Of course I think they are the cutest dogs on earth—except when they fight—but you be the judge. Meet my treasures, immortalized in fabric.

CUTTING

All measurements include ¼"-wide seam allowances.

From the green, cut:

1 strip, 1½" x 10½"

4 squares, 2½" x 2½"

From the black, cut:

2 strips, ¾" x 17"

2 strips, ¾" x 20½"

4 strips, 2¾" x 42"

From the brown for outer border, cut:

2 strips, 5½" x 17"

2 strips, 5½" x 21"

BLOCK ASSEMBLY

1. Copy or trace the foundation patterns from pages 58–68 onto foundation material. Make four copies *each* of parts A–E of the Dog Bone block and one copy *each* of the remaining patterns.

2. Referring to "How to Paper Piece" on page 7, paper piece the foundations for parts A–G of the Dog 1 block. Use the illustration as a guide for fabric placement. Join the parts as follows:

   Join A to B (AB).

   Join AB to C (ABC).

   Join D to E (DE).

   Join DE to F (DEF).

   Join DEF to G (DEFG).

   Join ABC to DEFG.

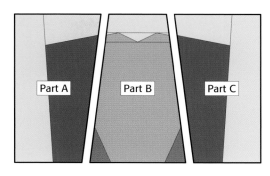
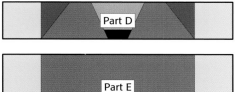

Dog 1

3. Paper piece the foundations for parts A–E of the Food Bowl block, referring to the illustration for fabric placement. Join the parts as follows:

   Join A to B (AB).

   Join AB to C (ABC).

   Join ABC to D (ABCD).

   Join ABCD to E.

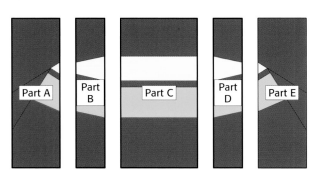

Food Bowl

4. Paper piece the foundations for parts A–G of the Dog 2 block, referring to the illustration for fabric placement. Part H is not foundation pieced; lay the foundation for part H on the wrong side of the appropriate fabric and cut out the triangle on the outer dashed lines. Discard the foundation. Join the parts as follows:

Join A to B (AB).

Join C to D (CD).

Join CD to E (CDE).

Join CDE to F (CDEF).

Join CDEF to G (CDEFG).

Join AB to CDEFG (ABCDEFG).

Join H to ABCDEFG.

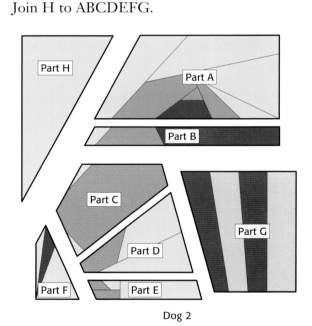

Dog 2

5. Paper piece the foundations for parts A–C of the NO! block, referring to the illustration for fabric placement. Join the parts as follows:

Join A to B (AB).

Join AB to C.

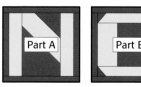

No!

6. Paper piece the foundations for parts A–J of the Dog 3 block, referring to the illustration for fabric placement. Join the parts as follows:

Join A to B (AB).

Join C to D (CD).

Join G to H (GH).

Join I to J (IJ).

Join CD to E (CDE).

Join AB to CDE (ABCDE).

Join ABCDE to F (ABCDEF).

Join ABCDEF to GH (ABCDEFGH).

Join ABCDEFGH to IJ.

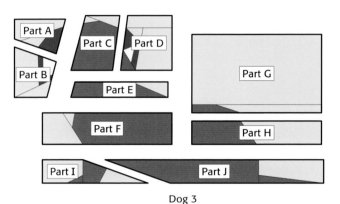

Dog 3

7. Use the sun patterns on page 63 and your favorite method to appliqué the sun to the upper right corner of the block. Stitch the green 1½" x 10½" strip to the bottom edge of the block.

8. Paper piece the foundations for parts A–F of the Dog 4 block, referring to the illustration on the facing page for fabric placement. Join the parts as follows:

Join A to B (AB).

Join C to D (CD).

Join E to F (EF).

Join AB to CD (ABCD).

Join ABCD to EF.

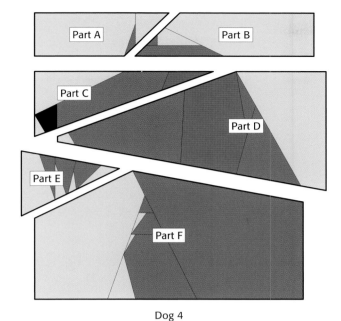

Dog 4

9. Stitch the four green 2½" squares together vertically to make the Paw block. Use the paw patterns on page 68 and your favorite method to appliqué one paw to each square, staggering them as shown.

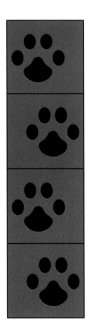

10. Paper piece the foundations for parts A–C of the Dog 5 block, referring to the illustration for fabric placement. Join the parts as follows:

   Join A to B (AB).

   Join AB to C.

Dog 5

11. Paper piece the foundations for parts A–E of the four Dog Bone blocks, referring to the illustration for fabric placement. For each block, join the parts as follows:

   Join A to B (AB).

   Join AB to C (ABC).

   Join ABC to D (ABCD).

   Join ABCD to E.

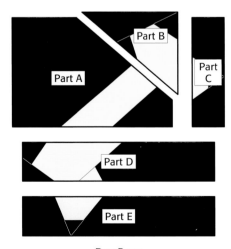

Dog Bone

Quilt-Top Assembly and Finishing

1. Stitch the Paw block to the right edge of the Dog 4 block. Arrange the blocks in two vertical rows as shown. Stitch the blocks in each row together, and then stitch the rows together.

2. Refer to the patterns and use your favorite appliqué method to make and apply the eyes to the Dog 1, Dog 4, and Dog 5 blocks.

3. Referring to "Adding Borders" on page 10 and the quilt assembly diagram, stitch the borders to the quilt top. For the inner border, sew the black ¾" x 20½" strips to the sides of the quilt top, and then sew the black ¾" x 17" strips to the top and bottom of the quilt top. For the outer border, sew the brown 5½" x 21" strips to the sides of the quilt top. Stitch the Dog Bone blocks to the ends of the brown 5½" x 17" strips, orienting the blocks as shown. Stitch the pieced border units to the top and bottom of the quilt top.

Quilt Assembly Diagram

4. Layer the quilt top with batting and backing; baste. Quilt in the ditch or as desired. Bind the quilt edges with the black 2¾"-wide strips.

- How could any dog lover not enjoy this welcome sign? Just make one regular image and one mirror image of the Dog 4 block foundation, add a strip of fabric between the two blocks, and appliqué the letters in place.

- Traditional blocks with plain centers, such as the Log Cabin and Star blocks shown here, are a great way to show off your favorite dog in a simple pillow.

- Pair a dog-print fabric with a couple of Dog Bone blocks and you have the makings of a fun place mat for your four-legged friend.

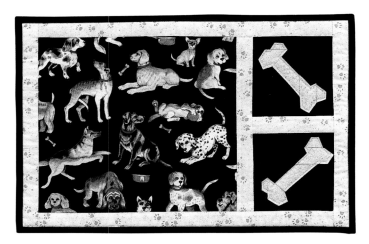

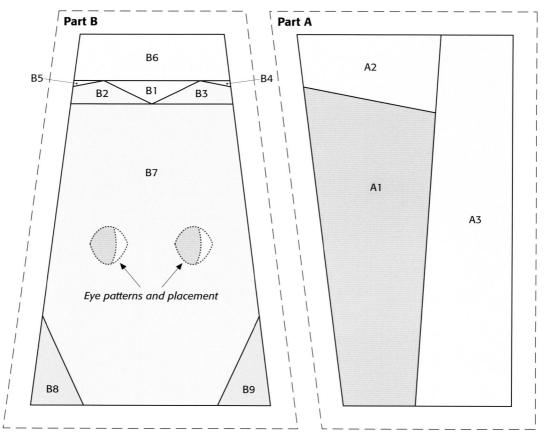

Part B

B6

B5 B4

B2 B1 B3

B7

Eye patterns and placement

B8 B9

Part A

A2

A1

A3

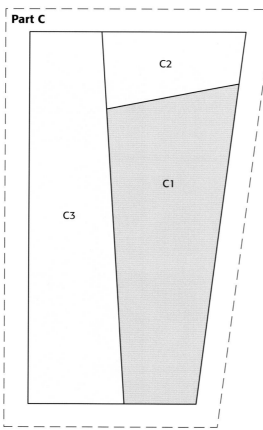

Part C

C2

C1

C3

**Dog 1 Block
Foundation Patterns**

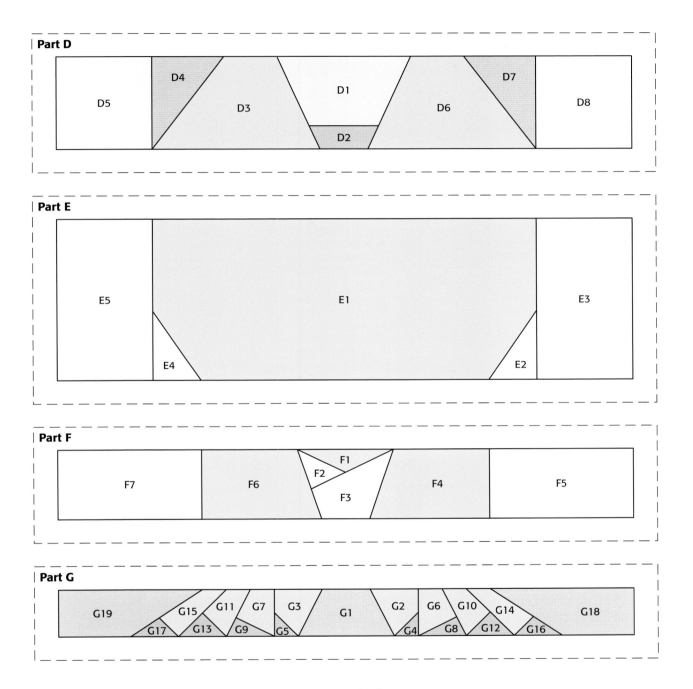

**Dog 1 Block
Foundation Patterns**

Part C

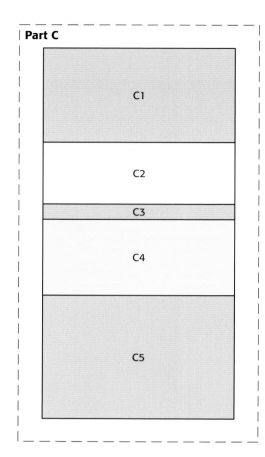

C1

C2

C3

C4

C5

Part B

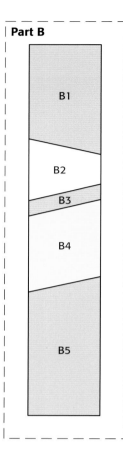

B1

B2

B3

B4

B5

Part A

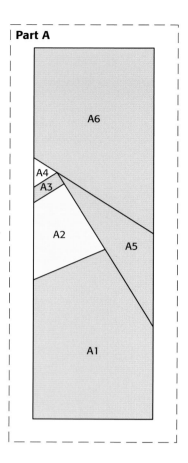

A6

A4

A3

A2

A5

A1

Part E

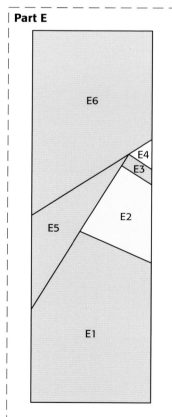

E6

E4

E3

E5

E2

E1

Part D

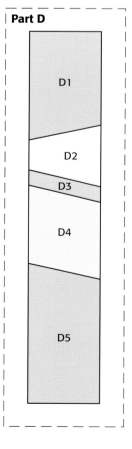

D1

D2

D3

D4

D5

**Food Bowl Block
Foundation Patterns**

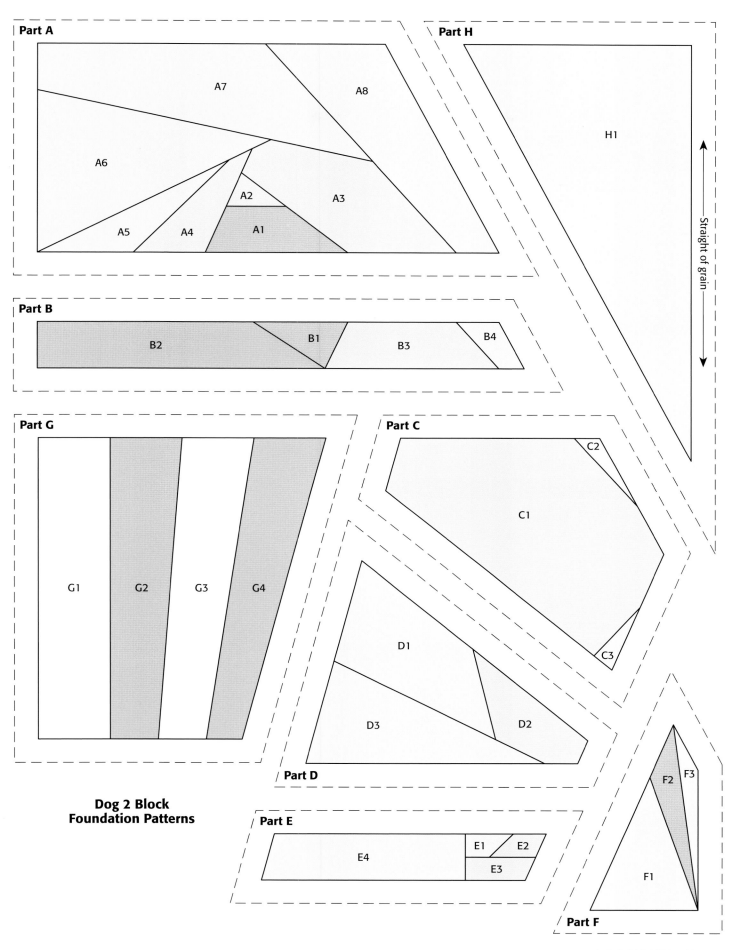

**Dog 2 Block
Foundation Patterns**

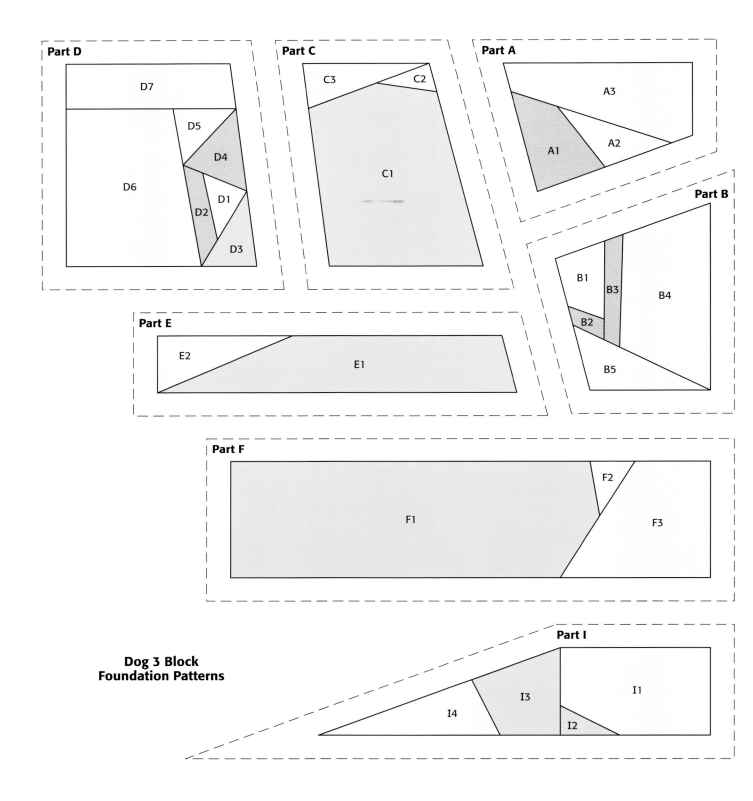

**Dog 3 Block
Foundation Patterns**

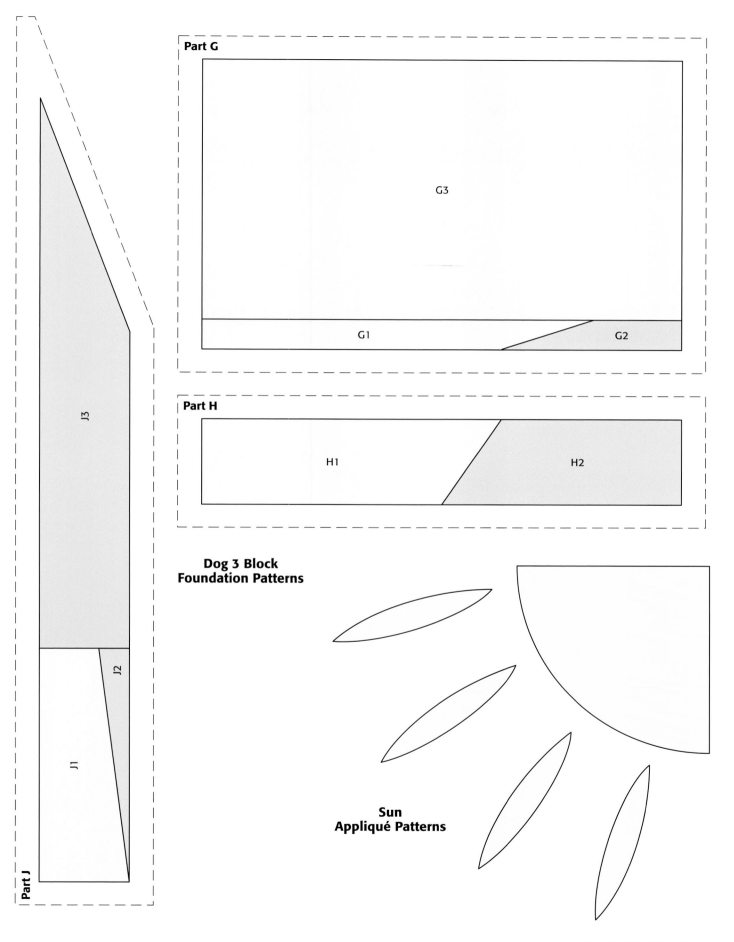

Part G

G3

G1 G2

Part H

H1 H2

**Dog 3 Block
Foundation Patterns**

Part J

J3

J2

J1

**Sun
Appliqué Patterns**

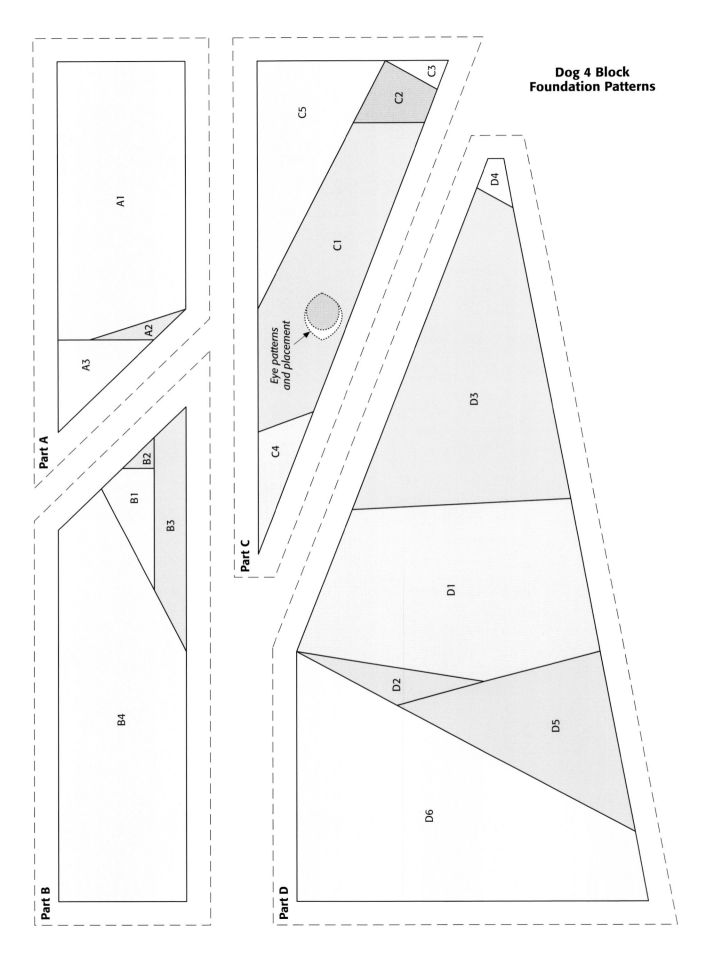

**Dog 4 Block
Foundation Patterns**

Part A

A1
A2
A3

Part B

B1
B2
B3
B4

Part C

C1
C2
C3
C4
C5

Eye patterns and placement

Part D

D1
D2
D3
D4
D5
D6

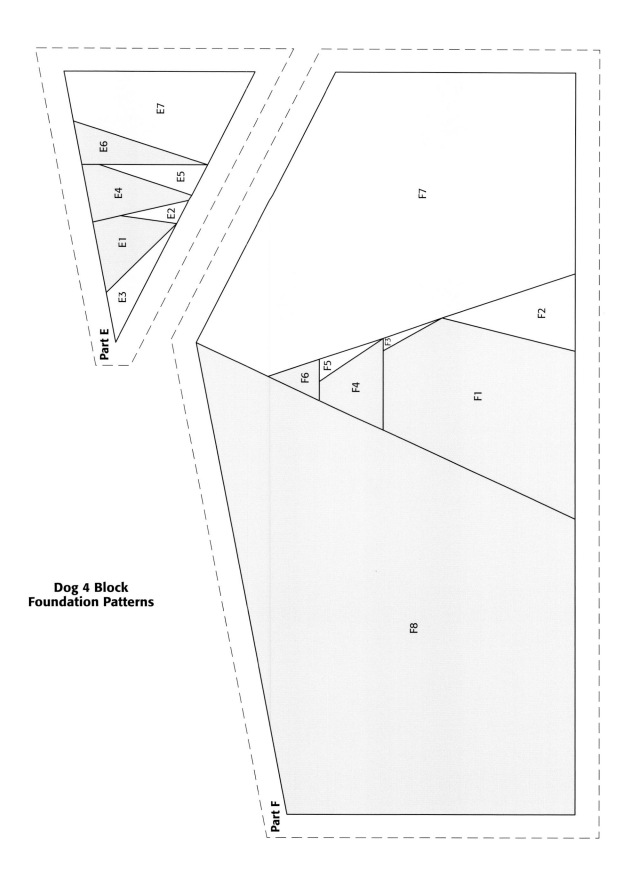

**Dog 4 Block
Foundation Patterns**

Part E

E7
E6
E5
E4
E2
E1
E3

Part F

F7
F2
F3
F5
F6
F4
F1
F8

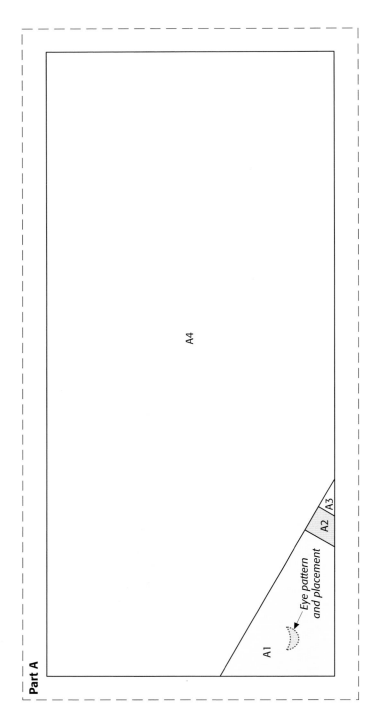

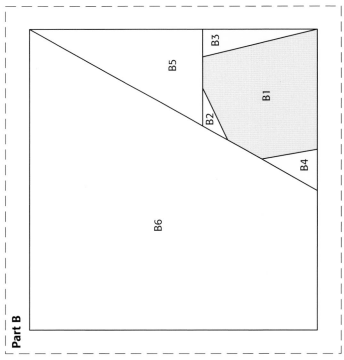

**Dog 5 Block
Foundation Patterns**

Part A

A4

A3
A2

A1

Eye pattern
and placement

Part B

B3
B5
B2
B1
B4
B6

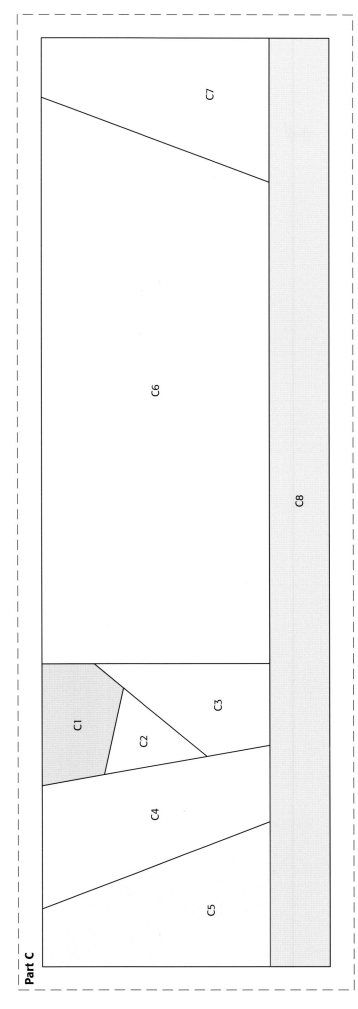

Part C

**Dog 5 Block
Foundation Pattern**

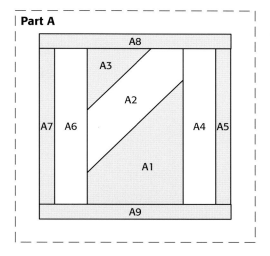

Part A

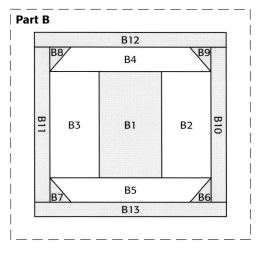

Part B

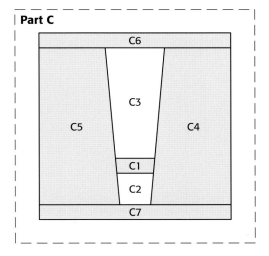

Part C

**No! Block
Foundation Patterns**

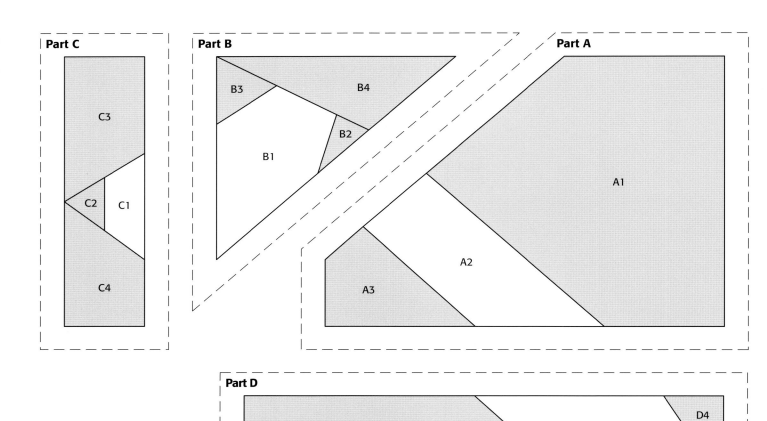

Part C

C3

C2 C1

C4

Part B

B3 B4

B2

B1

Part A

A1

A2

A3

**Dog Bone Block
Foundation Patterns**

Part D

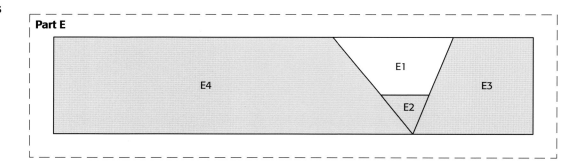

D1 D3 D4

D2 D5

Part E

E4 E1 E3

E2

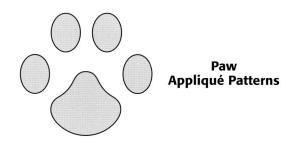

**Paw
Appliqué Patterns**

Finished quilt size: 13" x 31"
Finished block size: 6" x 6"

MATERIALS

Yardage is based on 42"-wide fabric.

- 1 yard of cream for background
- ½ yard of medium orange for inner border and binding
- ½ yard of dark orange for outer border
- ¼ yard of light green for turtle legs and heads
- Scraps of four different greens for turtle shells
- Scrap of black for eyes and mouth
- ⅝ yard of fabric for backing
- 17" x 35" piece of batting

CUTTING

All measurements include ¼"-wide seam allowances.

From the medium orange, cut:
2 strips, 1" x 6½"
2 strips, 1" x 25½"
3 strips, 2¾" x 42"

From the dark orange, cut:
2 strips, 3½" x 7½"
2 strips, 3½" x 31½"

As a child, I had pet turtles. They had such funny faces, and I loved to watch them. Although I don't have turtles anymore, thinking of the ones I had as a child makes me smile, so I wanted to create a quilt that features them.

BLOCK ASSEMBLY

1. Copy or trace the foundation patterns from pages 72–74 onto foundation material. Make two copies *each* of parts A and B of the Turtle 1 block and one copy *each* of parts A–C of the Turtle 2 and 3 blocks.

2. Referring to "How to Paper Piece" on page 7, paper piece the foundations for parts A and B of the two Turtle 1 blocks. Use the illustration as a guide for fabric placement. Choose a different green for each turtle's shell. Join part A to part B as shown for each block.

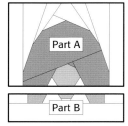

Turtle 1

3. Paper piece the foundations for parts A–C of the Turtle 2 block, referring to the illustration for fabric placement. Join the parts as follows:

   Join A to B (AB).

   Join AB to C.

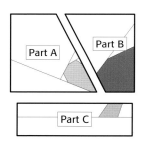

Turtle 2

4. Paper piece the foundations for parts A–C of the Turtle 3 block, referring to the illustration for fabric placement. Join the parts as follows:

   Join A to B (AB).

   Join AB to C.

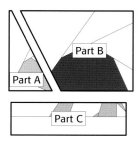

Turtle 3

QUILT-TOP ASSEMBLY AND FINISHING

1. Refer to the quilt assembly diagram to arrange the blocks in one vertical row. Stitch the blocks together.

2. Referring to the patterns, use your favorite appliqué method to make and apply the eyes to the Turtle 1 and Turtle 3 blocks, and the eyes and mouth to the Turtle 2 block.

3. Referring to "Adding Borders" on page 10 and the quilt assembly diagram, stitch the borders to the quilt top. For the inner border, sew the medium orange 1" x 6½" strips to the top and bottom of the quilt top, and then sew the medium orange 1" x 25½" to the sides of the quilt top. For the outer border, sew the dark orange 3½" x 7½" strips to the top and bottom of the quilt top, and then sew the dark orange 3½" x 31½" strips to the sides of the quilt top.

4. Layer the quilt top with batting and backing; baste. Quilt in the ditch or as desired. Bind the quilt edges with the medium orange 2¾"-wide strips.

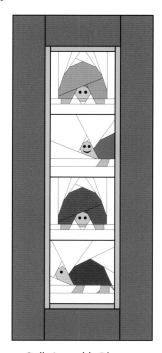

Quilt Assembly Diagram

❋ CREATIVE IDEAS ❋

- Use bright prints for the turtle's shells and you'll be guaranteed a great baby quilt!

- This table runner is sure to be popular if you have kids in the house!

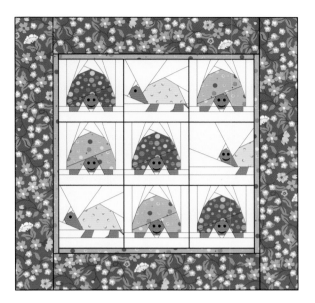

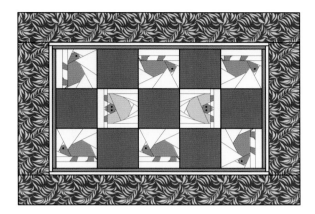

- Keep cold drafts out by placing this long pillow at the base of a door.

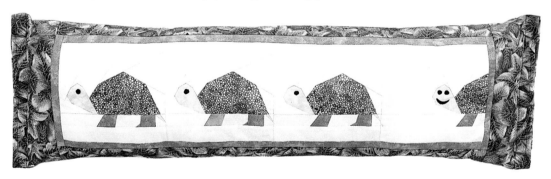

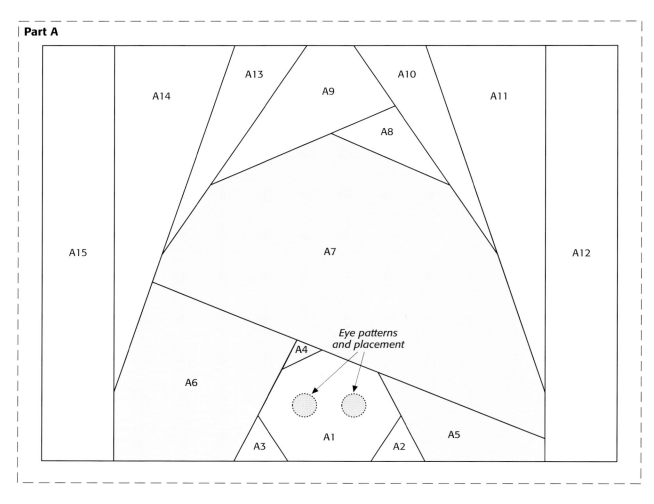

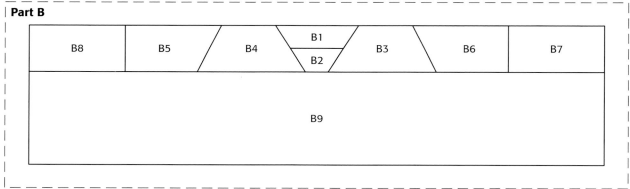

**Turtle 1 Block
Foundation Patterns**

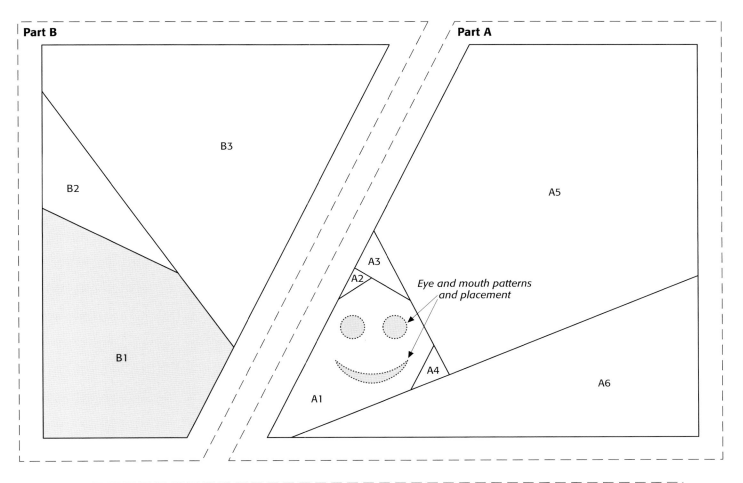

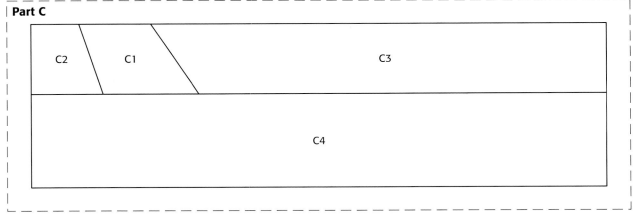

**Turtle 2 Block
Foundation Patterns**

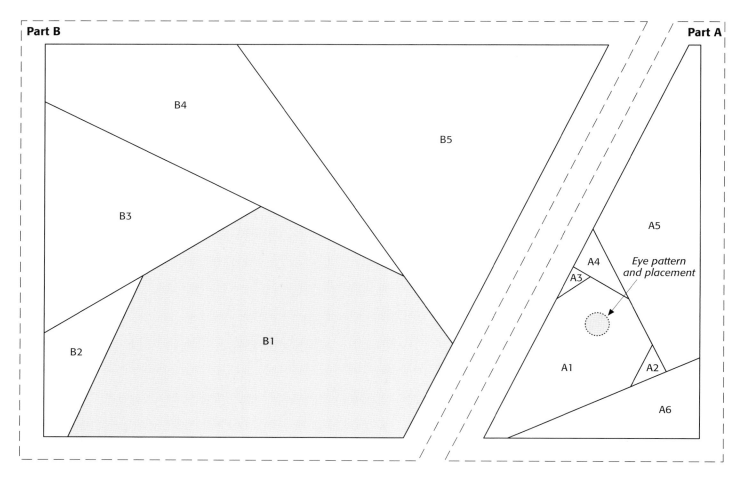

Part B

B4

B5

B3

B2

B1

Part A

A5

A4

A3

Eye pattern and placement

A1

A2

A6

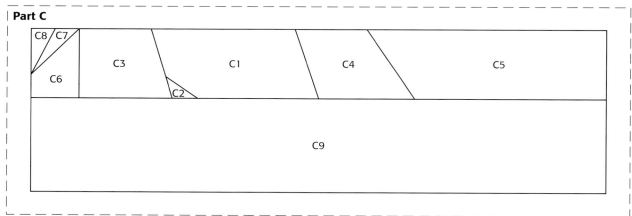

Part C

C8 / C7

C3

C1

C4

C5

C6

C2

C9

Turtle 3 Block
Foundation Patterns

Sometimes it's difficult to relax in this fast-paced world, but the playful cats in this wall hanging will teach you how to do it. Sit for a spell, watch the birds, and then take a nice, long stretch.

Finished quilt size: 17½" x 24½"
Finished Large Gray Cat block size: 6" x 12"
Finished Large Orange Cat block size: 12" x 8"
Finished Small Cat block size: 6" x 3"

MATERIALS

Yardage is based on 42"-wide fabric.

- 1¼ yards of blue for sky and middle border
- ¾ yard of brown for sashing, inner and outer borders, and binding
- ½ yard of medium orange for orange cats
- Scraps of assorted light oranges for orange cat's stripes, birds, and birdhouse
- Scraps of four different grays for gray cats and birdhouse hole
- Scrap of black for eyes and large gray and small orange cats' noses
- Scrap of pink for small gray cat's nose
- ⅞ yard of fabric for backing
- 22" x 29" piece of batting

CUTTING

All measurements include ¼"-wide seam allowances.

From the brown, cut:
2 strips, 1" x 12½"
2 strips, 1½" x 12½"
2 strips, 1" x 20½"
2 strips, 2½" x 14"
2 strips, 2½" x 25"
3 strips, 2¾" x 42"

From the blue, cut:
2 strips, ¾" x 13½"
2 strips, ¾" x 21"

BLOCK ASSEMBLY

1. Copy or trace the foundation patterns from pages 78–82 onto foundation material. Make one copy *each* of parts A–C of the Large Gray Cat block and parts A–I of the Large Orange Cat block. Make two copies of the Small Cat block; mark the paw placement on the foundation patterns.

2. Referring to "How to Paper Piece" on page 7, paper piece the foundations for parts A–C of the Large Gray Cat block. Use the illustration as a guide for fabric placement. Join the parts as follows:

   Join A to B (AB).

   Join AB to C.

3. Paper piece two Small Cat blocks, making one cat orange and the other cat gray. Refer to the illustration for fabric placement.

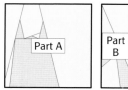

Large Gray Cat

Small Cat

4. Paper piece the foundations for parts A–I of the Large Orange Cat block, referring to the illustration for fabric placement. Join the parts as follows:

   Join A to B (AB).

   Join AB to C (ABC).

   Join ABC to D (ABCD).

   Join ABCD to E (ABCDE).

   Join G to H (GH).

   Join GH to I (GHI).

   Join F to GHI (FGHI).

   Join ABCDE to FGHI.

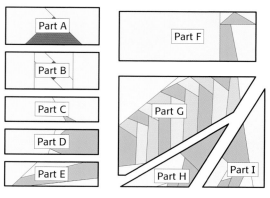

Large Orange Cat

❈ CREATIVE IDEA ❈

Create a simple table runner by bordering a cat print with blocks made from the Small Cat foundation pattern.

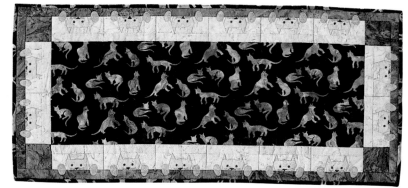

Quilt-Top Assembly and Finishing

1. Sew the blocks and the brown 1½" x 12½" strips together as shown.

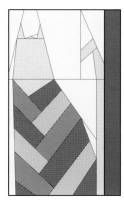
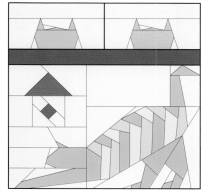

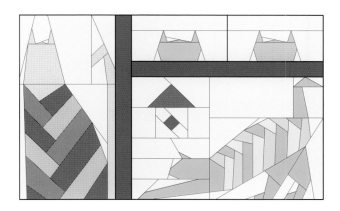

2. Referring to "Adding Borders" on page 10 and the quilt assembly diagram, sew the borders to the quilt top. For the inner borders, sew the brown 1" x 12½" strips to the sides of the quilt top, and then sew the brown 1" x 20½" strips to the top and bottom of the quilt top. For the middle border, sew the blue ¾" x 13½" strips to the sides of the quilt top, and then sew the blue ¾" x 21" strips to the top and bottom of the quilt top. For the outer border, sew the brown 2½" x 14" strips to the sides of the quilt top, and then sew the brown 2½" x 25" strips to the top and bottom of the quilt top.

3. Using your favorite appliqué method and the paw pattern on page 82, cut two paws *each* from the orange and gray fabrics that you used for the cats in the Small Cat blocks; appliqué the paws in place where indicated by the dotted lines on the pattern. The paws will overlap onto the brown strip below the Small Cat blocks. Referring to the patterns, use your favorite appliqué method to make and apply the eyes and noses to the Large Gray Cat block and the two Small Cat blocks. Machine straight stitch the whiskers to the Large Gray Cat block and the two Small Cat blocks and the eye and mouth to the Large Orange Cat block where indicated on the patterns. Set your machine for a narrow zigzag stitch and stitch the chain hanger to the birdhouse on the Large Orange Cat block where indicated on the pattern.

Quilt Assembly Diagram

4. Use the bird patterns on page 78 to cut two bird bodies and their corresponding wings from the desired fabrics. Appliqué the birds in place, using your favorite method and referring to the photo for placement.

5. Layer the quilt top with batting and backing; baste. Quilt in the ditch or as desired. Bind the quilt edges with the brown 2¾"-wide strips.

Part B

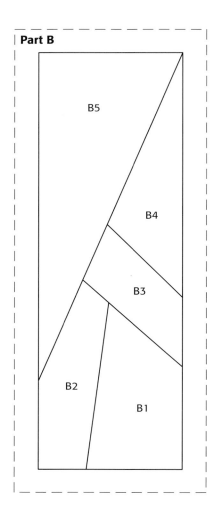

B5

B4

B3

B2

B1

Part A

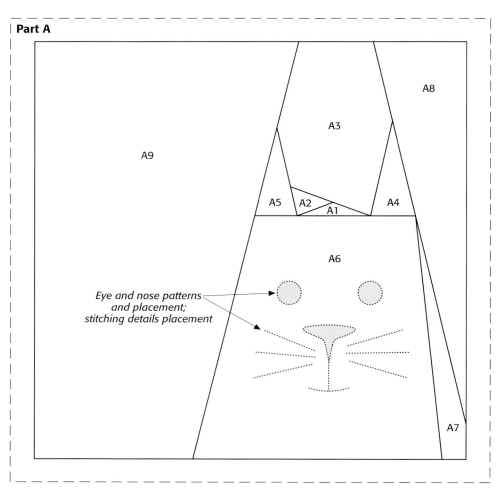

A8

A3

A9

A5   A2   A4

A1

A6

*Eye and nose patterns
and placement;
stitching details placement*

A7

**Large Gray Cat Block
Foundation Patterns**

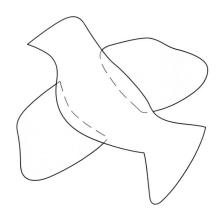
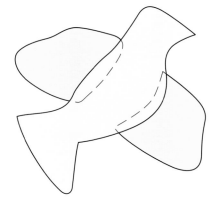

**Bird
Appliqué Patterns**

Part C

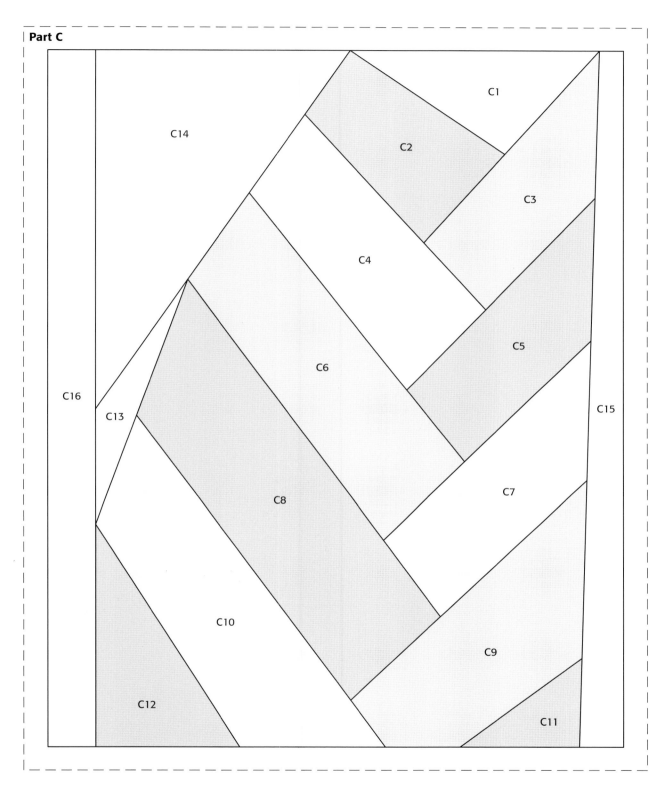

**Large Gray Cat Block
Foundation Pattern**

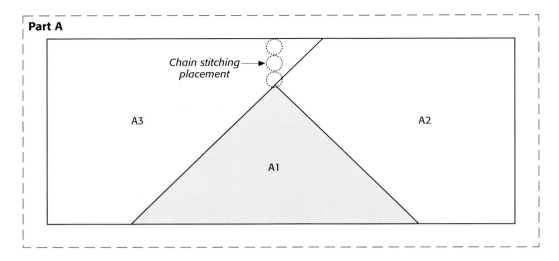

Part A

A3

A1

A2

Chain stitching placement

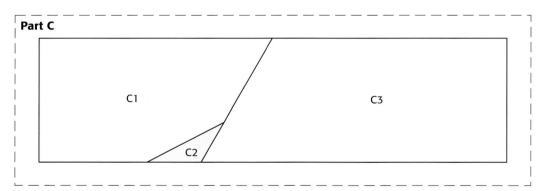

Part B

B6

B5

B2

B1

B3

B4

B7

**Large Orange Cat Block
Foundation Patterns**

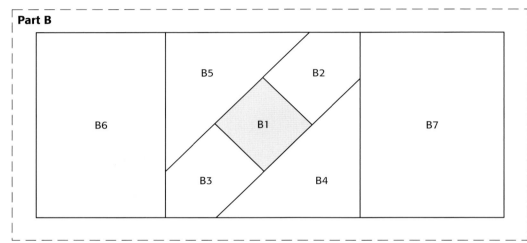

Part C

C1

C3

C2

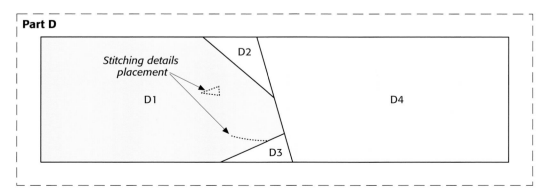

Part D

D2

D1

D4

D3

Stitching details placement

**Large Orange Cat Block
Foundation Patterns**

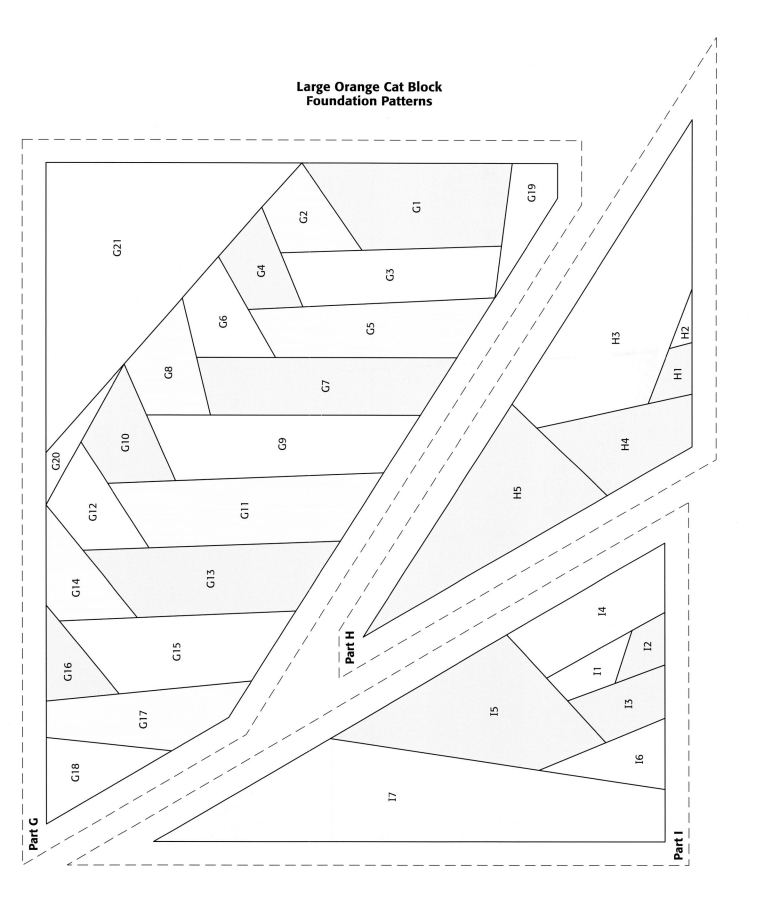

Part G

Part H

Part I

G1, G2, G3, G4, G5, G6, G7, G8, G9, G10, G11, G12, G13, G14, G15, G16, G17, G18, G19, G20, G21

H1, H2, H3, H4, H5

I1, I2, I3, I4, I5, I6, I7

Part F

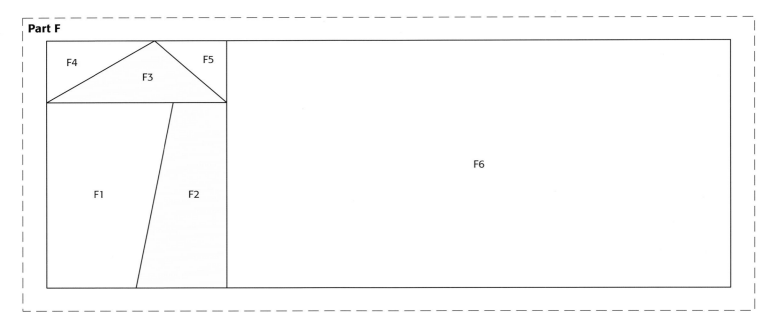

F4   F5
F3
F1   F2
F6

**Large Orange Cat Block
Foundation Patterns**

Part E

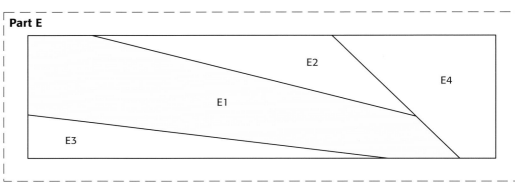

E2
E4
E1
E3

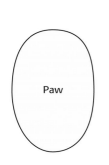

Paw

**Small Cat Block
Foundation and Appliqué Patterns**

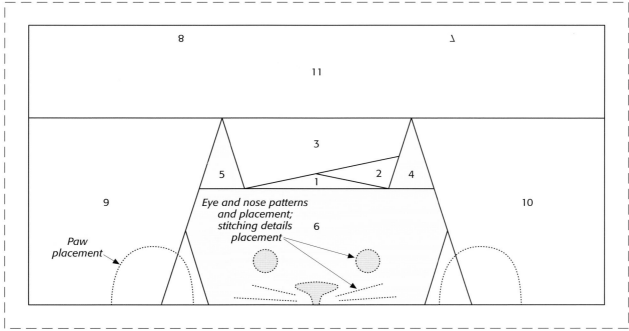

8   7
11
3
5   1   2   4
9   Eye and nose patterns
     and placement;
     stitching details
     placement   10
Paw
placement
6

Finished quilt size: 21" x 25"
Finished Tulip block size: 6" x 12"
Finished Flowerpot block size: 6" x 5"

MATERIALS

Yardage is based on 42"-wide fabric.

- 1 yard of cream for background
- ¾ yard of dark pink for tulips, middle border, and binding
- ⅝ yard of green for inner and outer borders
- ¼ yard of different green for stems and leaves
- Scraps of light and medium pink for tulips
- Scrap of dark gray for flowerpot
- Scrap of blue for flowerpot
- ⅞ yard of fabric for backing
- 25" x 30" piece of batting

CUTTING

All measurements include ¼"-wide seam allowances.

From the cream, cut:
1 strip, 1½" x 12½"
2 rectangles, 4" x 5½"

From the green for borders, cut:
2 strips, 1½" x 17½"
2 strips, 1½" x 15½"
2 strips, 3" x 20½"
2 strips, 3" x 21½"

From the dark pink, cut:
2 strips, 1" x 19½"
2 strips, 1" x 16½"
3 strips, 2¾" x 42"

Now this is a typical Dutch tulip . . . always askew! When tulips are in the growing process they are straight, but this never lasts very long. Even after only one day in a vase they'll collapse a bit, but there is an old Dutch trick that will have them straight in no time. Do you know it? Use a straight pin to pierce a little hole all the way through the flower's stem, just under each tulip's head. After a few hours, they'll be straight as a pole again!

Block Assembly

1. Copy or trace the foundation patterns from pages 86–90 onto foundation material one time each.

2. Referring to "How to Paper Piece" on page 7, paper piece the foundations for parts A–C of the Tulip 1 and Tulip 2 blocks. Use the illustrations as a guide for fabric placement. Join the parts for each block as follows:

   Join A to B (AB).

   Join AB to C.

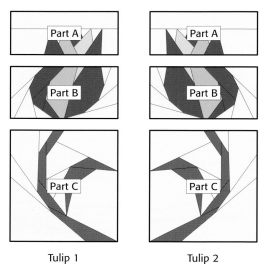

Tulip 1   Tulip 2

3. Paper piece the Flowerpot block, referring to the illustration for fabric placement.

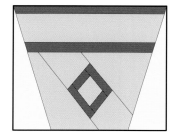

Flowerpot

Quilt-Top Assembly and Finishing

1. Stitch the blocks and the cream strip and rectangles together as shown above right.

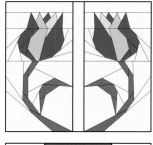

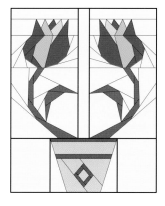

2. Referring to "Adding Borders" on page 10 and the quilt assembly diagram, sew the borders to the quilt top. For the inner border, sew the green 1½" x 17½" strips to the sides of the quilt top, and then sew the green 1½" x 15½" strips to the top and bottom of the quilt top. For the middle border, sew the dark pink 1" x 19½" strips to the sides of the quilt top, and then sew the dark pink 1" x 16½" strips to the top and bottom of the quilt top. For the outer border, sew the green 3" x 20½" strips to the sides of the quilt top, and then sew the green 3" x 21½" strips to the top and bottom of the quilt top.

Quilt Assembly Diagram

3. Layer the quilt top with batting and backing; baste. Quilt in the ditch or as desired. Bind the quilt edges with the dark pink 2¾"-wide strips.

- Make two sets of Tulip blocks and stitch them together end to end for a lovely table runner.

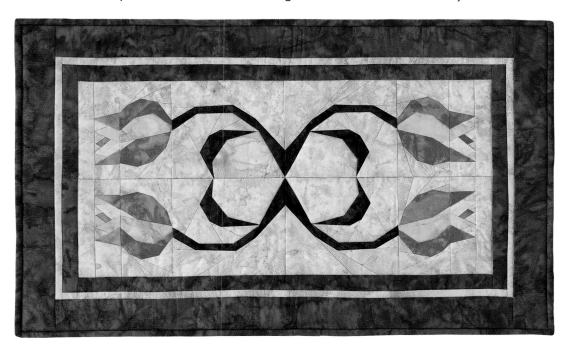

- Combine the Tulip blocks with the 6" Windmill blocks from "Dutch Windmills" on page 12 for a double Dutch treat.

- Make an elegant wall hanging from a trio of tulips.

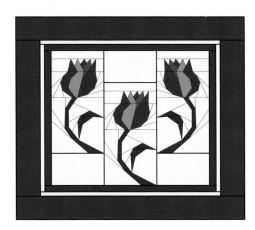

Part A

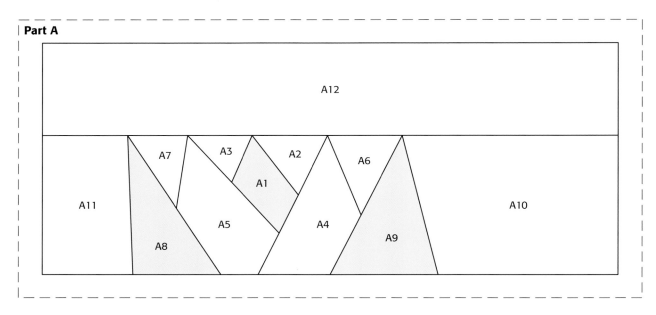

Part B

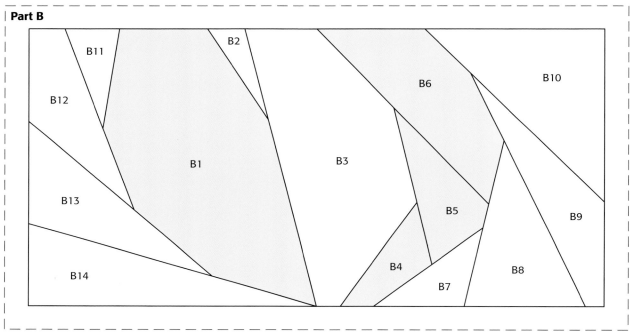

**Tulip 1 Block
Foundation Patterns**

Part C

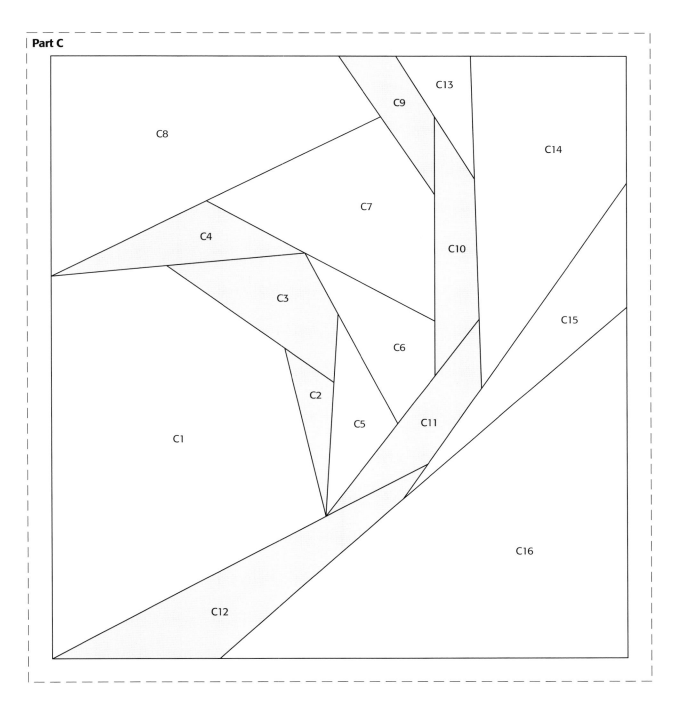

C8

C9

C13

C14

C7

C4

C10

C3

C6

C2

C5

C11

C15

C1

C16

C12

**Tulip 1 Block
Foundation Pattern**

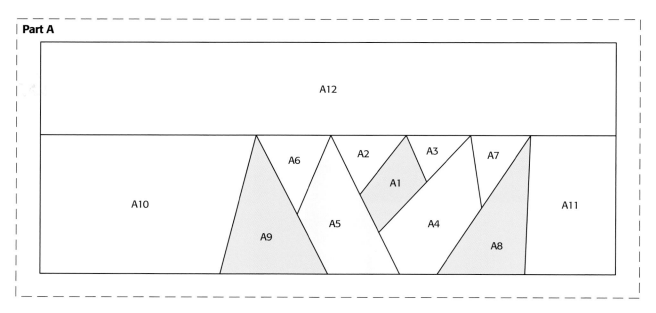

Part A

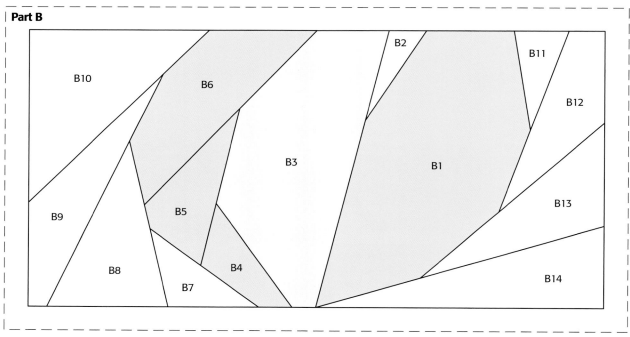

Part B

**Tulip 2 Block
Foundation Patterns**

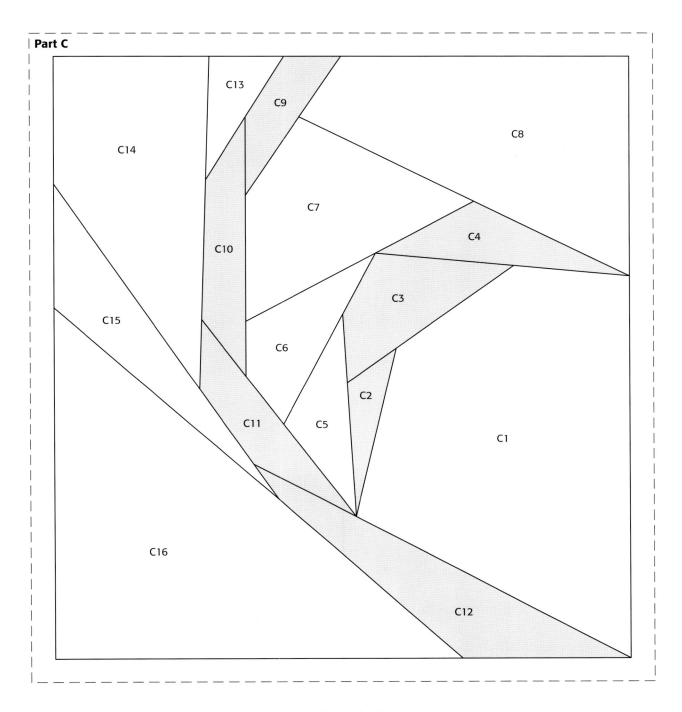

Part C

C13
C9
C8
C14
C7
C4
C10
C3
C15
C6
C2
C11
C5
C1
C16
C12

**Tulip 2 Block
Foundation Pattern**

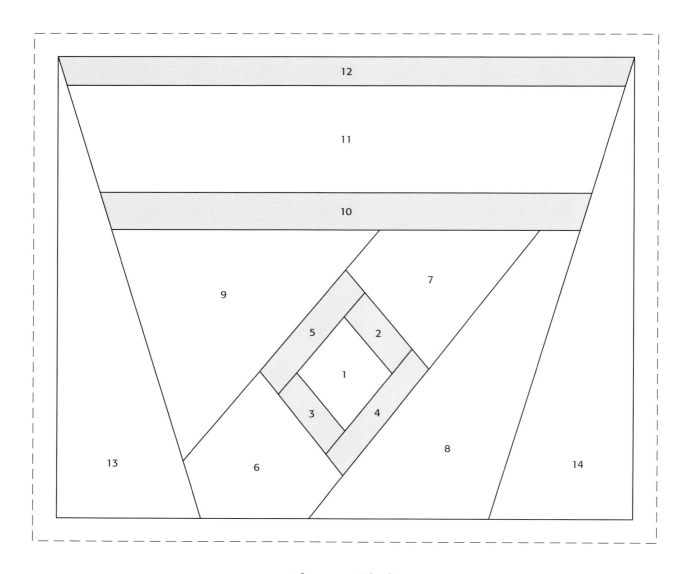

Flowerpot Block
Foundation Pattern

When I see teddy bears, my mind jumps back to the bear I used to have when I was a child. He was soft and woolly, with a sweet face and ears that would listen to all of my little-girl secrets. I tucked him along wherever I went and would panic when I couldn't find him immediately! This is a charming quilt for children, but also for those who haven't really grown up. Admit it—it's hard not to love a teddy bear.

Finished quilt size: 33" x 42"
Finished block size: 7" x 7"

MATERIALS

Yardage is based on 42"-wide fabric.

- 1¾ yards of blue for background
- ¾ yard of dark red for sashing squares, pieced-border corner blocks, and binding
- ¾ yard of dark brown for pieced-border inner and outer strips and corner blocks
- ⅝ yard of light brown for sashing and pieced-border middle strip and corner blocks
- Scraps of 12 assorted browns, at least 12" x 16", for teddy bears
- Scraps of 12 assorted browns, at least 8" x 8", for teddy bear snouts and inner ears
- Scraps of assorted prints for collars
- Scrap of black for eyes and noses
- 1½ yards of fabric for backing
- 37" x 46" piece of batting

CUTTING

All measurements include ¼"-wide seam allowances.

From the light brown, cut:
17 strips, 2½" x 7½"
2 strips, 1½" x 25½"
2 strips, 1½" x 34½"

From the dark red, cut:

6 squares, 2½" x 2½"

5 strips, 2¾" x 42"

From the dark brown, cut:

2 strips, 1½" x 25½"

2 strips, 1½" x 34½"

2 strips, 2½" x 25½"

2 strips, 2½" x 34½"

BLOCK ASSEMBLY

1. Copy or trace the foundation patterns from pages 94 and 95 onto foundation material. Make 12 copies *each* of parts A–C of the Teddy Bear block and 4 copies of the Border Corner block.

2. Referring to "How to Paper Piece" on page 7, paper piece the foundations for parts A–C of each Teddy Bear block. Use the illustration as a guide for fabric placement. Join the parts for each block as follows:

   Join A to B (AB).

   Join AB to C.

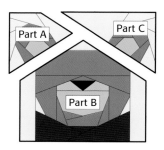

Teddy Bear

3. Referring to the pattern, use your favorite appliqué method to make and apply the eyes to each Teddy Bear block. Machine straight stitch the mouth where indicated on the pattern. Refer to the project photo on page 91 for different mouth variations to make each bear unique, if desired.

4. Paper piece the foundations for the four Border Corner blocks, referring to the illustration for fabric placement.

Border Corner

QUILT-TOP ASSEMBLY AND FINISHING

1. To make the block rows, alternately stitch three Teddy Bear blocks and two light brown 2½" x 7½" strips together, beginning and ending with a block. Make four rows.

Make 4.

2. To make the sashing rows, alternately stitch three light brown 2½" x 7½" strips and two dark red 2½" squares together, beginning and ending with a strip. Make three rows.

Make 3.

3. Refer to the quilt assembly diagram to alternately stitch the block rows and the sashing rows together, beginning and ending with a block row.

4. Referring to "Adding Borders" on page 10 and the quilt assembly diagram on the facing page, stitch the pieced border to the quilt top. To make the pieced-border units, sew a dark brown 1½" x 34½" strip and a dark brown 2½" x 34½" strip to the sides of each light

brown 1½" x 34½" strip as shown. Repeat with the 25½"-long strips.

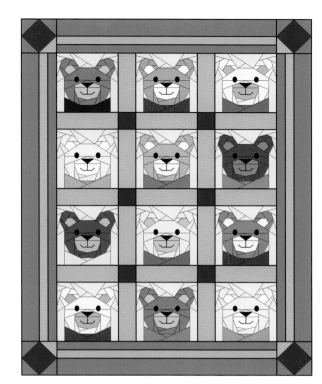

5. Refer to the quilt assembly diagram to stitch the 34½"-long units to the sides of the quilt top. Stitch the Border Corner blocks to each end of the remaining units, orienting the blocks as shown so that the light brown corner is toward the inside of the quilt. Stitch the units to the top and bottom edges of the quilt top.

6. Layer the quilt top with batting and backing; baste. Quilt in the ditch or as desired. Bind the quilt edges with the dark red 2¾"-wide strips.

Quilt Assembly Diagram

✲ CREATIVE IDEAS ✲

- Make your own coasters from the Border Corner block pattern. They make a quick and lovely gift.

- When I ran across a very attractive bear-print fabric, I just couldn't resist making it into a handy tote bag, complete with a Teddy Bear block flap. The Teddy Bear block could also be quilted and bound, and then sewn onto a tote bag for use as a pocket. Or even use it on top of a fabric-covered folder. Plenty of possibilities!

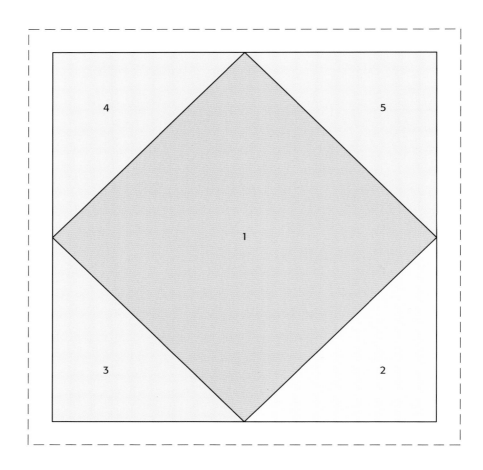

**Border Corner Block
Foundation Pattern**

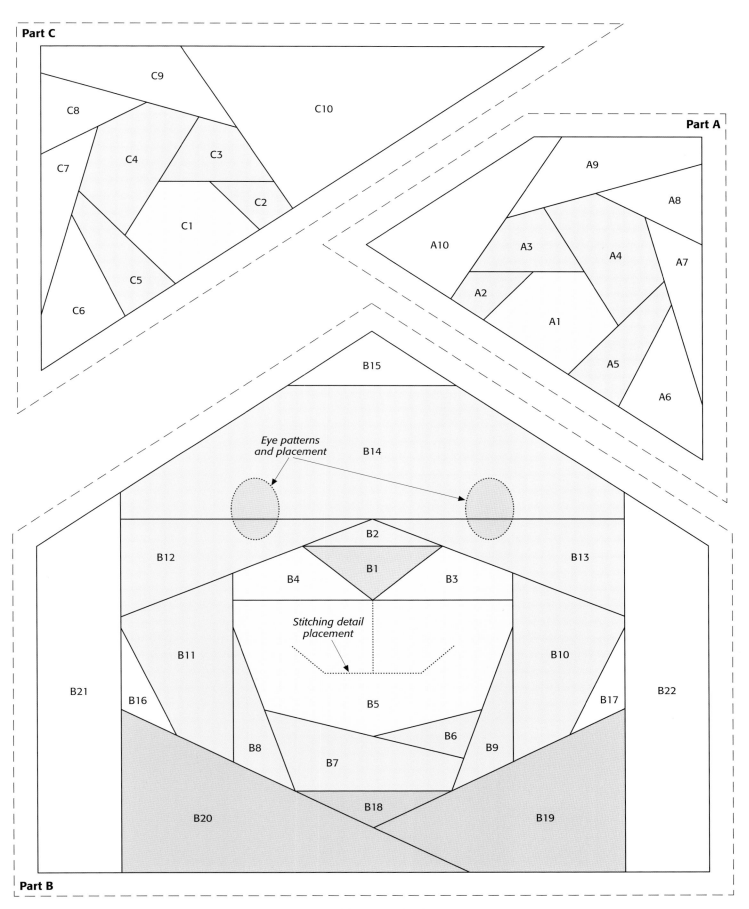

**Teddy Bear Block
Foundation Patterns**

❀ ABOUT THE AUTHOR ❀

Wendy Vosters was attracted to crafting at an early age. She learned how to knit, embroider, crochet, and make dolls. Her mom, who never ever sits still, set the example. Wendy had her first sewing machine at the age of 13 and started to make her own clothes—no, not the ordinary clothes you saw everywhere, but ones embellished with cross-stitches, ribbons, and appliqués. She even made a very fine cutwork blouse for her granny, who always wore the garment with pride.

Wendy finished high school and continued to craft and make her own wardrobe, even while attending the Maastrichter Conservatory of Music (yes, she is a lecturing musician). Her love of quilting was born in 1995 during a quilt show in the vicinity. She took a beginning quiltmaking class and hasn't stopped quilting yet! Nowadays, she makes several patterns for various patchwork shops in the Netherlands. Most of them are paper-piecing patterns, of course.

Wendy is happily married to Piet and lives with him, her mom, and four dogs in a town in the southern part of the Netherlands. Fortunately her mom is a very enthusiastic quilter as well, so they are never short of topics for conversation. Piet is often out on the sea fishing, so this leaves Wendy plenty of time for her favorite pastime—quilting! Visit Wendy's Web site at www.wendyvosters.com.